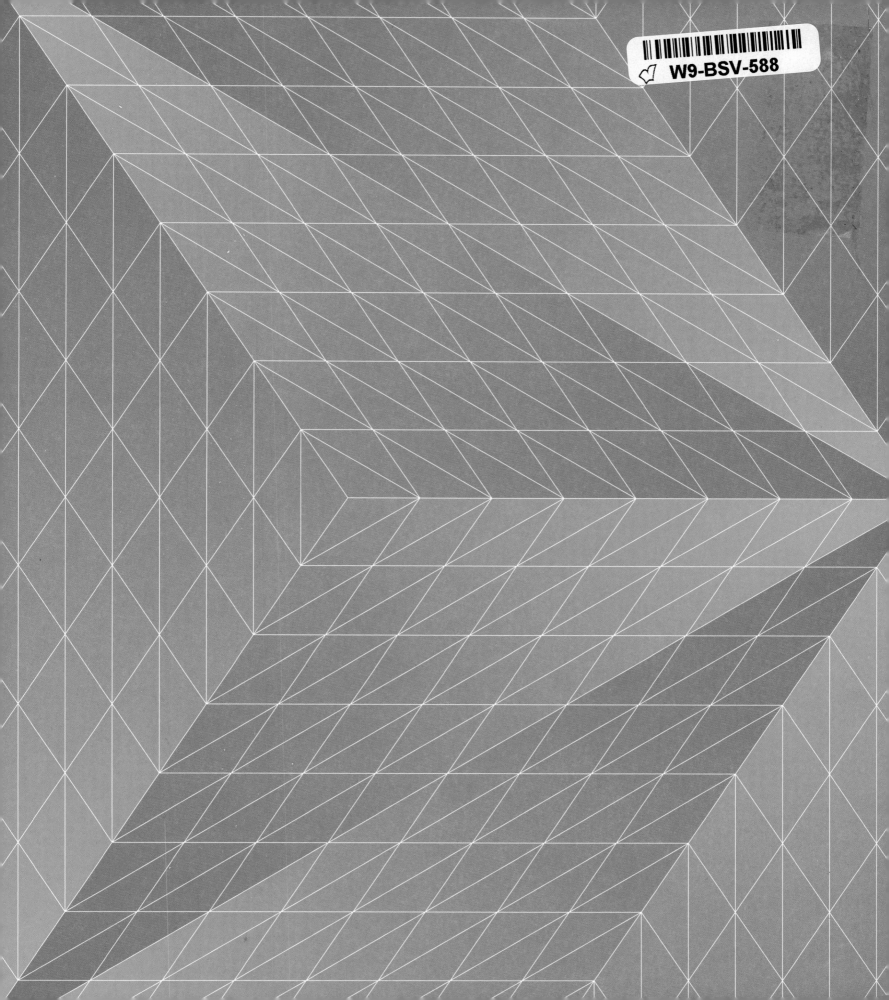

Predators

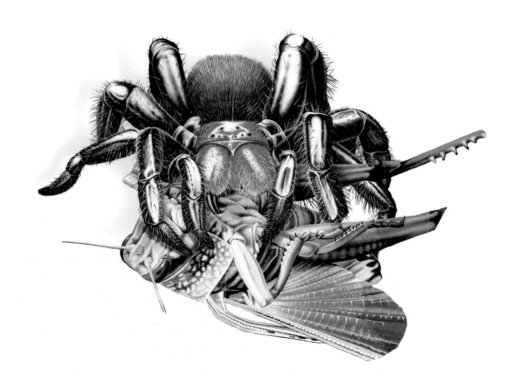

SIMON & SCHUSTER BOOKS FOR YOUNG READERS
An imprint of Simon & Schuster Children's Publishing Division
1230 Avenue of the Americas, New York, New York 10020

Conceived and produced by Weldon Owen Pty Ltd
61 Victoria Street, McMahons Point
Sydney, NSW 2060, Australia

Group Chief Executive Officer John Owen
President and Chief Executive Officer Terry Newell
Publisher Sheena Coupe
Creative Director Sue Burk
Concept Development John Bull, The Book Design Company
Editorial Coordinator Mike Crowton
Vice President, International Sales Stuart Laurence
Vice President, Sales and New Business Development Amy Kaneko
Vice President, Sales: Asia and Latin America Dawn Low
Administrator, International Sales Kristine Ravn

Editor Helen Flint
Designers Julie Brownjohn and Gabrielle Green
Cover Designers Gaye Allen and Kelly Booth

Color reproduction by Chroma Graphics (Overseas) Pte Ltd
Printed by SNP Leefung Printers Ltd
Manufactured in China

A WELDON OWEN PRODUCTION

Library of Congress Cataloging-in-Publication Data
Seidensticker, John.
Predators / John Seidensticker and Susan Lumpkin.
p. cm. — (Insiders)
Includes index.

ISBN-13: 978-1-4169-3863-7 (hardcover)
ISBN-10: 1-4169-3863-X (hardcover)

1. Predatory animals—Juvenile literature. 2. Predation (Biology)—Juvenile literature.
I. Lumpkin, Susan. II. Title.
QL758.S45 2008
591.5'3—dc22
2007061741

Predators

John Seidensticker and Susan Lumpkin

Simon & Schuster Books for Young Readers
New York   London   Toronto   Sydney

Contents

introducing

The Cycle of Life

A World of Predators   8

Killers of the Past   10

Lost to the World: Extinct   12

Prey Fighting Back   14

Natural Weapons

Beaks and Teeth   16

Claws and Talons   18

Fangs and Venom   20

Size and Strength   22

Life in the Fast Lane: Speed   24

Killer Instinct

Deadly Teamwork   26

Hiding and Traps   28

Carnivorous Plants   30

Killer Senses   32

Creative Killers   34

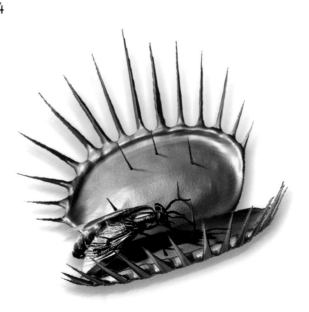

 *focus*

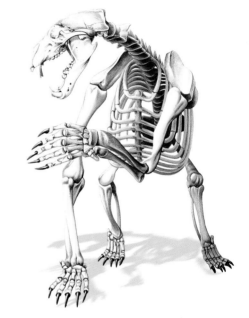

Top of the Food Chain

Supreme Hunters: Cats   38

Towers of Strength: Bears   40

Wild Dogs and Wolves   42

Kings of the Sea: Sharks   44

Crocodiles and Alligators   46

Flying High: Birds of Prey   48

Predator Habitats

Under the Canopy: Rain Forests   50

The Heat of the Sun: Deserts   52

Above and Below the Ice: Polar   54

Under the Sea: Coral Reefs   56

Across the Plains: Grasslands   58

Diverse Predators   60

Glossary   62

Index   64

troducing

A World of
Predators

Predators are nature's killers: animals that live by eating other animals. When we think of predators, we tend to think of animals that fear no others, such as lions or sharks. These species are at the very top of the food chain. But nearly all animals are predators, whether they feed on the tiniest krill or a mighty buffalo. Herbivores—animals that live on plants alone—are called primary consumers, while at the bottom of the food chain are producers, such as bacteria, plants, or algae, that create their own food from sunlight and carbon dioxide. The higher a species is in the food chain, the fewer individuals of that species exist. That is why it is easy to see many deer in the forest, but much harder to spot even a single wolf.

Eat and be eaten

Animals at the top of the food chain, called top predators, eat other animals, but no other animals usually eat them. In the middle of the chain are animals that both eat and are eaten by other animals.

Shark to shrimp
A bull shark catches mainly large fish, while fish often snap up shrimp. Shrimp feast on tiny plants, animals, and bits of dead material.

Ocean food pyramid
Abundant green plants, called phytoplankton, are at the bottom of the ocean food pyramid. Rarer animals, like sharks, are at the top.

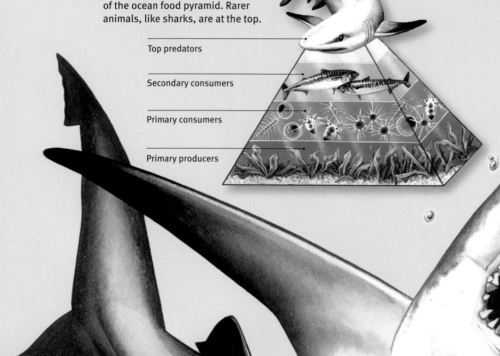

Top predators

Secondary consumers

Primary consumers

Primary producers

Eagle to mouse
A short-toed eagle snatches a meal of grass snake, but this top predator also eats mammals such as rabbits. A seed- and insect-eating harvest mouse satisfies the grass snake.

Puma to skink *A hungry puma may kill and eat a raccoon, which eats various foods, including this five-lined skink and other lizards, fruits, and berries.*

Killers of the Past

The largest predators of all time were some species of dinosaurs. One of the largest was called *Giganotosaurus*, which means "giant southern lizard." This monster lived in South America about one hundred million years ago. It weighed around eight tons (7.1 t) and was three car lengths long. These huge predators needed to eat a lot of food. Among their prey was another dinosaur called *Argentinosaurus*. The biggest dinosaur found so far, *Argentinosaurus* was probably the largest land animal that ever lived. This plant-eating reptile weighed 70 tons (63.5 t) or more and was 115 feet (35 m) long. It traveled in groups of about 20 animals.

Terrible teeth
Tyrannosaurus was long thought to be the largest predatory dinosaur to have existed. Its teeth were the size and shape of a banana.

Down for the count
Here, two *Giganotosaurus* attack an *Argentinosaurus*. The huge predators probably slashed and bit their even bigger prey until it collapsed. This is how African wild dogs take down prey much larger than themselves.

Rudder tail *Its slender, long tail may have helped* Giganotosaurus *keep its balance while making quick turns to the left and right—an important skill for keeping up with the defensive turns of its prey.*

PAST PREDATORS

Now-extinct predators had many adaptations for hunting and killing in the air, on land, and in the ocean that are similar to the adaptations of modern predators.

Jaws Up to 80 feet (25 m) long, the aquatic reptile *Liopleurodon* raced through ancient seas sniffing out and gulping down any creature it could catch in its jaws.

Fearsome flyers Immense flying reptiles called pterosaurs once swooped down to snatch fish from lakes, rather like bald eagles do today.

Pack hunters The size of a wolf, and with a similar set of teeth, *Cynognathus* was a speedy reptilian carnivore. Like wolves, they hunted in packs.

Bloodhound *The shape of the skull shows that a large area of its brain was devoted to sniffing out prey.*

Awesome teeth *Teeth serrated like a bread knife and, at eight inches (20 cm), about as long as a bread knife's blade let* Giganotosaurus *slice skin off its prey.*

Slashers Giganotosaurus *had three fingers on each hand, each tipped with a long, sharp claw. It probably used these to slash and wound prey.*

Lost to the World
Extinct

Predators do not hunt their prey to extinction. If they did, they would go extinct themselves. But there is one big exception: humans. Our dietary flexibility, mobility, and technology have enabled us to escape extinction, even when our prey went extinct. As our prey disappeared, we switched to other food, moved to other places where prey was abundant, and used technology—including domestication of livestock as well as better tools—to find and kill prey. As predators, we also compete with other predators for space and food, and as the human population grows ever larger, all species are losing ground to people. Many have already vanished from Earth.

Haast's giant eagle This now-extinct species was the largest eagle to have ever lived.

Moa This large, flightless bird from New Zealand was hunted to extinction.

Domino effect The first humans to live in New Zealand hunted moas for food, sending all 10 species of these huge flightless birds to extinction within 100 years. Soon after that, Haast's giant eagles, which relied on moas for their own sustenance, followed them into extinction.

Passenger pigeon *When Europeans reached North America, they found billions of passenger pigeons living in flocks miles wide. The last bird died in a zoo in 1914.*

Dodo *Dodos went extinct in 1681, 80 years after Dutch sailors found them on Mauritius, a then-uninhabited island in the Indian Ocean. The big birds made a tasty meal for passing sailors.*

Great auk *Flightless, and therefore easy to hunt for food, the great auk was last seen in Newfoundland, Canada, in 1852.*

Giant tortoise *Native to tropical islands, some species are already extinct; all others are endangered. People hunt these big, slow-moving reptiles for their meat and eggs.*

Steller's sea cow *This immense, 26-foot (7.9-m)- long animal was discovered in 1741 and hunted to extinction in fewer than 30 years.*

Going, going, gone

In the last 500 years, 22 reptile species, 70 mammals, 80 fish, and 135 birds have gone extinct, many because of human predation. And it is getting worse. Today, more than 340 reptiles and 1,000 each of mammal, fish, and bird species are threatened with extinction.

Bison *Millions of bison roamed the Great Plains of the American West in the early 1800s. Within 75 years, only a handful remained. Conservation programs have helped bison numbers recover, but cannot restore the vast herds of the past.*

Tiger *The last few thousand tigers left in Asia are being poached for their fur and a diverse array of other body parts used in traditional Asian medicine. Without protection, tigers will soon be extinct.*

Colobus monkey *Conservationists declared Miss Waldron's red colobus monkey extinct in the year 2000, just 67 years after the West African animals were first seen by scientists.*

Cod *After a century of human overfishing, these staples of fish and chips are no longer caught for commercial sale. Even with protection, cod may never exist in large numbers again.*

Prey
Fighting Back

Predators use many ways to find and kill their meals, just as prey have many clever approaches to keep themselves from being eaten. Some prey run very fast or use weapons of their own, such as stingers or sharp hooves, to attack a threatening predator. Others mimic those species that have weapons or are poisonous. Still more sport colors and shapes that blend into the environment so that predators cannot easily see them. Living in groups gives some prey the strength of numbers to better detect or deter predators. Hiding is a simple way to fight back, but it works.

Strength in numbers
Animals that work together to protect themselves from predators form defensive groups. Often the animals are of the same species, but sometimes, different creatures work together to the benefit of both.

Big bodyguards *Oxpecker birds ride around on the backs of buffalo, using the buffalo's big bodies to shield themselves from predators.*

On duty *A guard force of tiny leaf-cutter ant soldiers, with ferocious biting jaws, protects the larger ants that are toting food to their nest.*

Powerful mandibles

CIRCLING THE WAGONS

When wolves threaten, musk oxen form a tight defensive ring, with their formidable horns facing the predators. This protects their vulnerable young—and their own unarmed rear ends.

Shell game *Hermit crabs hide in empty shells to avoid octopuses and other predators. Flowery anemones growing on the shells may provide camouflage as well.*

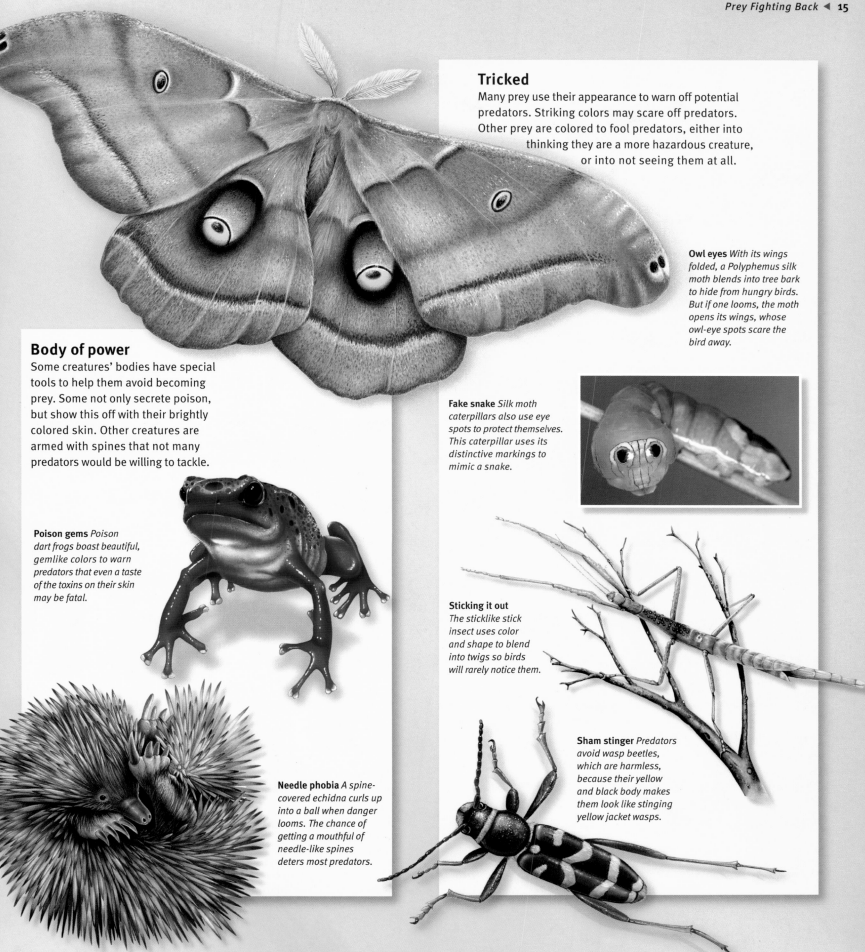

Tricked

Many prey use their appearance to warn off potential predators. Striking colors may scare off predators. Other prey are colored to fool predators, either into thinking they are a more hazardous creature, or into not seeing them at all.

Owl eyes *With its wings folded, a Polyphemus silk moth blends into tree bark to hide from hungry birds. But if one looms, the moth opens its wings, whose owl-eye spots scare the bird away.*

Body of power

Some creatures' bodies have special tools to help them avoid becoming prey. Some not only secrete poison, but show this off with their brightly colored skin. Other creatures are armed with spines that not many predators would be willing to tackle.

Fake snake *Silk moth caterpillars also use eye spots to protect themselves. This caterpillar uses its distinctive markings to mimic a snake.*

Poison gems *Poison dart frogs boast beautiful, gemlike colors to warn predators that even a taste of the toxins on their skin may be fatal.*

Sticking it out *The sticklike stick insect uses color and shape to blend into twigs so birds will rarely notice them.*

Sham stinger *Predators avoid wasp beetles, which are harmless, because their yellow and black body makes them look like stinging yellow jacket wasps.*

Needle phobia *A spine-covered echidna curls up into a ball when danger looms. The chance of getting a mouthful of needle-like spines deters most predators.*

Beaks and
Teeth

Predatory mammals, reptiles, and fish all use their teeth to catch, kill, or eat prey. But not all teeth are the same. They come in different shapes, sizes, and strengths, and do different jobs—such as gripping, stabbing, slicing, crushing, grinding, and tearing. Some predators, such as cats, have different teeth for different jobs. Others, such as crocodiles, have only one all-purpose type of tooth. Birds have no teeth at all. Predatory birds use their beak as a substitute for teeth to catch, kill, and eat their prey. And like teeth, beaks vary among bird species and are specialized for different jobs.

ENDLESS SUPPLY

All sharks have a big mouthful of sharp teeth set in rows four teeth deep or more. Sharks often break their teeth, so they are always growing new ones.

Tiger shark Sharp teeth shaped like can openers for opening sea turtle shells

Blue shark Triangular teeth with serrated edges for stabbing and tearing flesh from fish

Great white Sharp and finely serrated cutting teeth for slicing thick-skinned animals such as seals

Short-fin mako Long, sharp, pointed, and curved teeth for stabbing speedy fish

Killer canines *A tiger uses its canines, which are as long as an adult's finger, to crush the neck vertebrae of smaller prey, or to clamp down on the throat of large prey until it suffocates.*

All sorts
Birds use their beaks for many functions, including defense, preening, and hunting. Beaks vary greatly in size and shape, depending on the food that a bird eats.

Scissor blades *The bladelike fourth premolars on the upper jaw, called carnassials, and the first molars on the lower jaw work like scissors to shear meat off bones.*

By hook or by crook
Hawks catch prey in their talons, then tear off bite-size chunks of flesh with their strong, hooked beak.

Slice and dice A tern's long, scissor-like beak catches small fish and slices them into pieces that it swallows whole.

Open wide *A tiger's wide gape lets it get its mouth firmly around the neck of large prey, such as a deer or wild cattle.*

Scoop and sieve
A flamingo's curved beak holds a scoop of water. The water is filtered out through a sievelike structure in its beak. It then swallows any small sea creatures left inside.

The rasp *A tiger's tongue is covered with tiny, hooklike bumps, or papillae, that rasp every last bit of meat from a bone.*

Chisel and harpoon
A woodpecker bores through dead wood with a chisel-shaped beak and pokes around with its tongue. The sharp-tipped tongue harpoons any grubs it finds.

Making room *This toothless gap makes room for the canines to bite deep into prey.*

Toolbox of teeth

Tigers, like all cats, have several different kinds of teeth, each with a different function. Sharp, stout canines kill. Small front incisors pluck feathers or fur. Cheek teeth—premolars and molars—shear meat off bones and cut and tear it into chunks.

Incisor

Canine

Molar

Under the skin

A tiger's 30 teeth are set in short, powerful jaws, which are attached to a short, robust skull and large jaw muscles.

Claws and
Talons

Predators use their claws and talons to capture or kill prey, either alone or in combination with teeth. In vertebrates, such as mammals and birds, claws and talons on the tips of their toes are special versions of the nails on human fingers and toes. Tigers and lions use their claws to strengthen their grasp on prey or to slash rivals. Bears hold food in their claws and use them to dig out prey living underground. Birds of prey, such as eagles and owls, snatch up and pierce a meal in their talons. Some invertebrates, such as shellfish and spiders, have claws that are modified legs to hold, cut, or crush prey.

Head game
Apart from its fearsome talons, the owl has other specialized parts that work together to make it an awesome predator.

Eyes forward Forward-facing eyes give owls binocular vision, which helps them judge the precise distance to their prey.

Multipurpose beak An owl crushes prey in its strong beak to kill it, then tears it apart with the hooked tip.

About face An owl's neck has 14 vertebrae, which enable it to turn its head all the way around to spot prey.

CLAWS BIG AND SMALL

When we think of claws, we tend to think of the fearsome grizzly bear, but many other creatures use specialized claws to hunt their prey.

Finger tool The aye-aye, a primate from Madagascar, probes tree holes for insect larvae with an extra-long finger tipped with a long claw.

Double claws A lobster crushes a prawn in its crusher claw and tears it apart with the smaller, sharper pincer claw. Lobster claws are modified legs.

Sound mufflers *A fringe of comblike feathers on the leading edges of an owl's primary wings muffles the sound of air rushing past the swooping bird so its prey cannot hear it coming.*

In the grasp

Swooping down, an owl extends its powerful legs and feet, which end in four toes tipped with sharp, curved talons on each foot. Its toes and talons close around prey such as moles and let the owl carry its meal away.

Relaxed grip *A special locking mechanism in an owl's feet lets the bird hold on to prey, even for hours, without toe muscle effort.*

Talons *When an owl attacks prey, its talons are spread out wide to increase the chance of a successful strike.*

Fangs and
Venom

Many animals use poisons or venoms to capture or kill prey and deter predators. Being poisonous is a defense against predators, while being venomous is both defense and offense. Eating or touching a poisonous animal, such as a poison dart frog or a fugu, may be fatal. But venomous species, such as scorpions and some snakes, actively inject their victims with deadly toxins using fangs, spines, stingers, or other special structures. Venomous predators use their toxic bite or sting to paralyze and kill prey and to attack predators—as well as unsuspecting people who chance upon them. Some shrews puncture prey's skin with their teeth so their toxic saliva can do its work.

Assorted needles

A snake's fangs are teeth that work like hypodermic needles to inject venom. The fangs of different species of snakes have different designs.

Fold-away
The long fangs of some species fold backward into the mouth and unfold to strike.

At the ready Some snakes have short, hollow front fangs that are always in position to strike.

In the rear
Fangs set in the rear of a snake's jaw have grooves that venom flows through.

LIFE-SAVING SERUM

Doctors inject medicine, called antivenin, to treat human victims of venomous snakebites and scorpion stings. Antivenins neutralize the toxins in venom that affect the nervous system or destroy tissue.

2 The venom is given to a horse in gradually increasing doses.

1 Venom is "milked" from a scorpion's (or snake's) venom gland.

3 The horse produces antivenin in its blood, which is collected and used to treat humans.

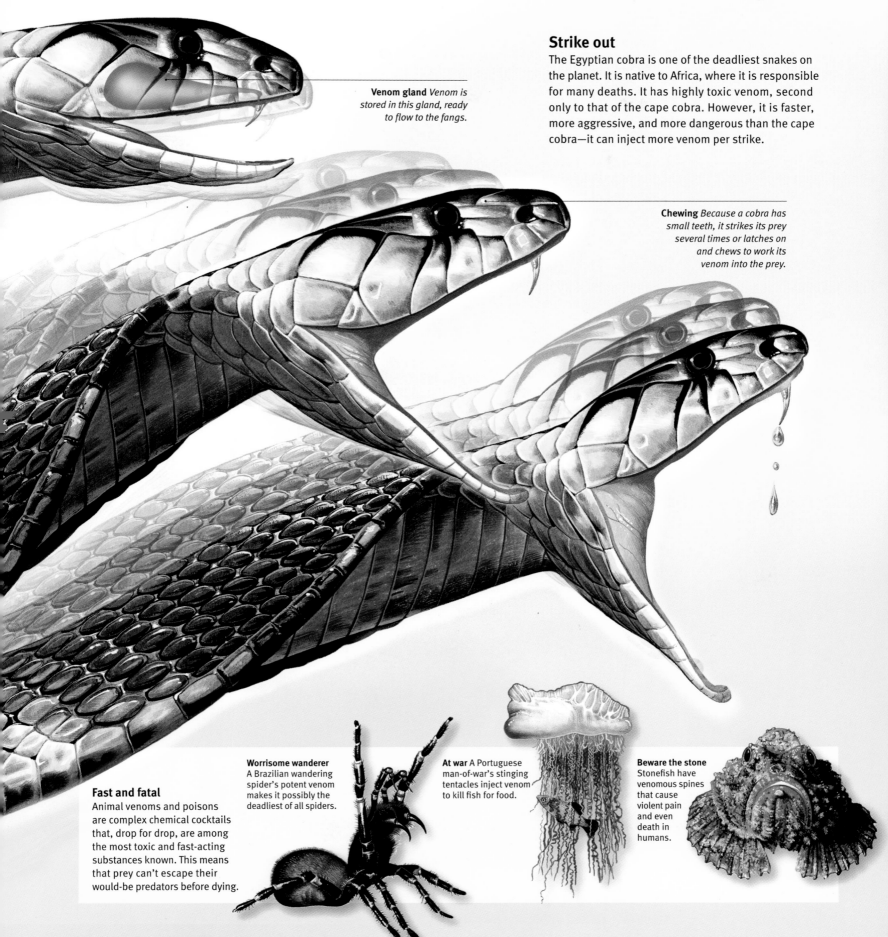

Venom gland *Venom is stored in this gland, ready to flow to the fangs.*

Strike out

The Egyptian cobra is one of the deadliest snakes on the planet. It is native to Africa, where it is responsible for many deaths. It has highly toxic venom, second only to that of the cape cobra. However, it is faster, more aggressive, and more dangerous than the cape cobra—it can inject more venom per strike.

Chewing *Because a cobra has small teeth, it strikes its prey several times or latches on and chews to work its venom into the prey.*

Fast and fatal
Animal venoms and poisons are complex chemical cocktails that, drop for drop, are among the most toxic and fast-acting substances known. This means that prey can't escape their would-be predators before dying.

Worrisome wanderer
A Brazilian wandering spider's potent venom makes it possibly the deadliest of all spiders.

At war A Portuguese man-of-war's stinging tentacles inject venom to kill fish for food.

Beware the stone
Stonefish have venomous spines that cause violent pain and even death in humans.

Size and
Strength

Sheer size and strength, not fancy weapons or high speed, give some predators an edge over their prey. Constrictor snakes do not bother with venom—they use their strong muscles to squeeze prey to death. Chimpanzees are strong enough to kill prey such as monkeys by hurling them against the ground. In other cases, a particular kind of size or strength is key. Hyenas are not very big, but the immense power of their jaws lets them crunch bones that would break the teeth of other carnivores. Great size and strength also make some potential prey safe from predators. For instance, nothing preys on adult elephants.

Tight squeeze

An anaconda kills large prey, such as a baby tapir, by coiling its muscular body around the victim and squeezing it to death. Every time the prey exhales, the snake squeezes tighter, keeping the prey from inhaling. The prey soon suffocates.

TITANIC BATTLE

The largest living predators, sperm whales, reach 60 feet (18 m) in length and 50 tons (45 t) in weight. Their immense size enables them to take on giant squid, which measure more than 40 feet (12 m) from tail to tentacle tip.

Big tooth With teeth measuring 7 inches (18 cm) in length, sperm whales boast the largest teeth on the planet.

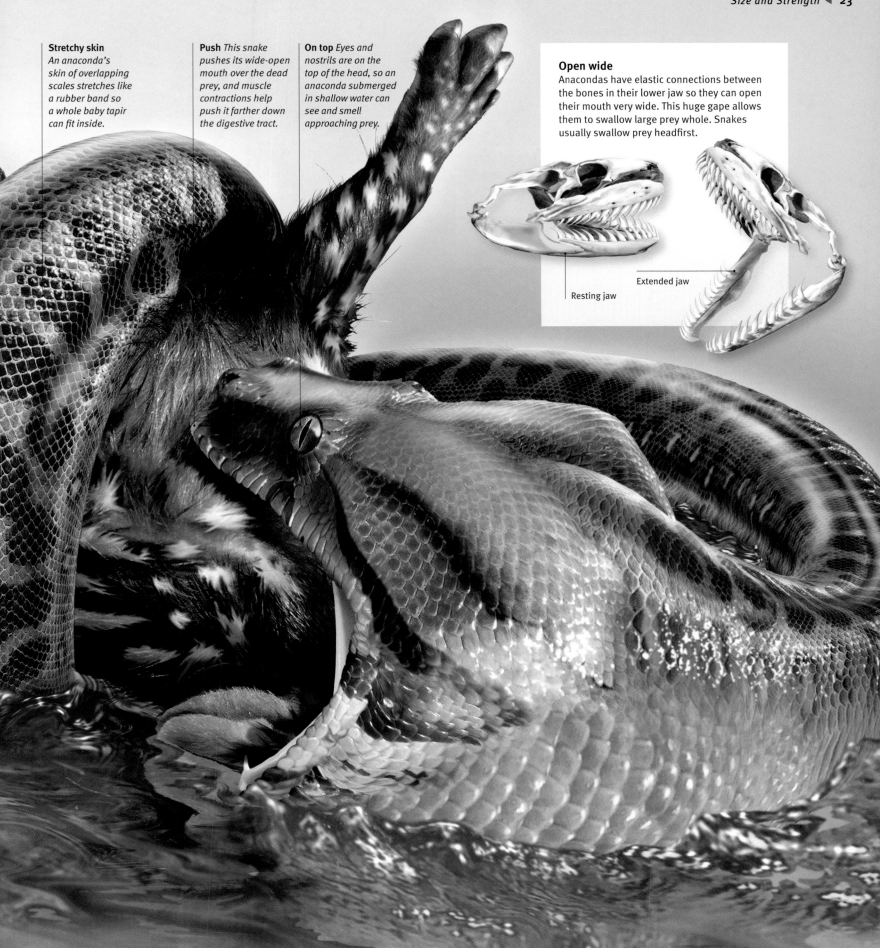

Stretchy skin
An anaconda's skin of overlapping scales stretches like a rubber band so a whole baby tapir can fit inside.

Push *This snake pushes its wide-open mouth over the dead prey, and muscle contractions help push it farther down the digestive tract.*

On top *Eyes and nostrils are on the top of the head, so an anaconda submerged in shallow water can see and smell approaching prey.*

Open wide
Anacondas have elastic connections between the bones in their lower jaw so they can open their mouth very wide. This huge gape allows them to swallow large prey whole. Snakes usually swallow prey headfirst.

Resting jaw

Extended jaw

Life in the Fast Lane
Speed

Speed kills. In the world of predators and prey, the prize often goes to the fastest. Predators win when they can outrun or accelerate more quickly than their prey. Speed can also kill prey directly, because a blow delivered at high speed is more deadly than one delivered slowly—the difference between a punch and a touch. When we think of speedy animals, we usually think of fairly large creatures running, flying, or swimming fast. But the speed of individual body parts—such as legs kicking or jaws closing—is often more important, especially for some of the smallest predators.

Animal Olympians
The world's fastest human sprinter boasts a top speed of about 27 miles per hour (43.5 km/h), which is slow compared with the peregrine falcon, the fastest bird; the cheetah, the fastest land mammal; and the sailfish, the fastest fish in the sea.

Amazing acceleration *A sprinting cheetah reaches 45 miles per hour (72 km/h) in 2.5 seconds and may then reach 64 miles per hour (103 km/h). Very fast acceleration, not speed alone, is what enables a cheetah to overtake speedy prey.*

Sailing through the sea *A sailfish races into a school of fish at 68 miles per hour (110 km/h). At that speed, the impact of its long bill hitting a fish kills the prey, much like the impact of a speeding car hitting a person.*

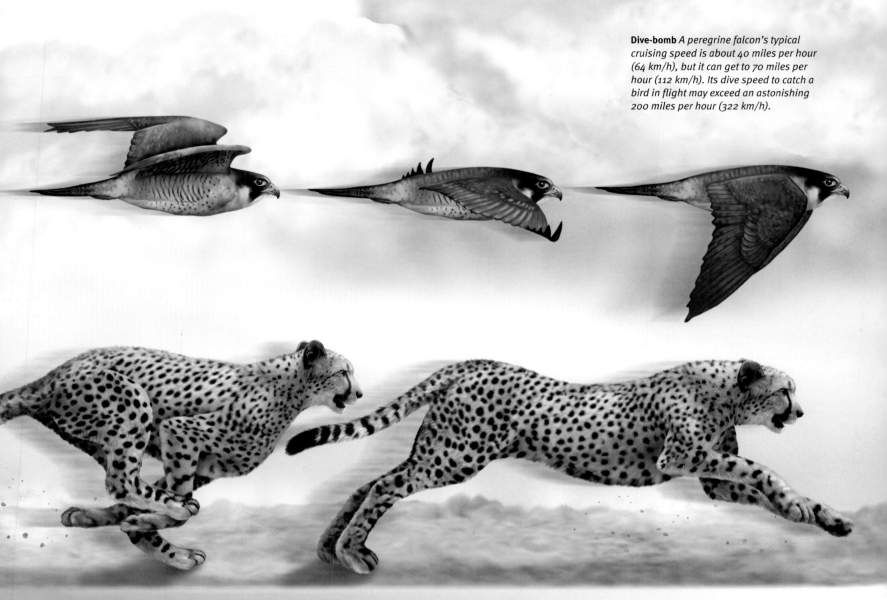

Dive-bomb *A peregrine falcon's typical cruising speed is about 40 miles per hour (64 km/h), but it can get to 70 miles per hour (112 km/h). Its dive speed to catch a bird in flight may exceed an astonishing 200 miles per hour (322 km/h).*

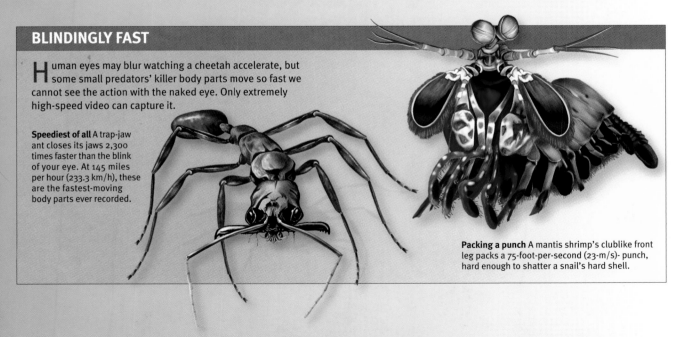

BLINDINGLY FAST

Human eyes may blur watching a cheetah accelerate, but some small predators' killer body parts move so fast we cannot see the action with the naked eye. Only extremely high-speed video can capture it.

Speediest of all A trap-jaw ant closes its jaws 2,300 times faster than the blink of your eye. At 145 miles per hour (233.3 km/h), these are the fastest-moving body parts ever recorded.

Packing a punch A mantis shrimp's clublike front leg packs a 75-foot-per-second (23-m/s)- punch, hard enough to shatter a snail's hard shell.

Deadly
Teamwork

Many predators find strength in numbers. Individually, an ant is no match for a grasshopper, but by attacking in droves, they can kill a creature that is thousands of times larger than they are. Beyond overpowering prey simply by assaulting it in force, some wily species form hunting groups that use a coordinated strategy to gain the upper hand. Surprisingly, individuals of two different species sometimes team up. Moray eels chase prey out of the nooks and crannies of a coral reef to be snapped up by grouper fish, while prey fleeing into the coral to escape the groupers are devoured by the eels. On the flip side, living in groups helps some prey evade predators.

Working as one

Ants are voracious predators that attack and subdue prey larger than themselves with fierce bites and venomous stings. Ants also assemble in large numbers and use the same weapons to drive off their own attackers and intruders.

POD CASTING

Groups, or pods, of dolphins hunt cooperatively for their fish prey. One member of a dolphin pod swims in circles around a school of fish, herding the fish toward other hungry dolphins waiting for their next meal.

Team killers
African wild dogs live and hunt in close-knit packs, working together to catch prey much larger than themselves. Packs can chase escaping prey at up to 37 miles per hour (60 km/h).

Good feeling
Ants have poor eyesight. Feelers, or antennae, are their main sensory organs.

Stinger *The stinger, which comes out of an ant's tail end, injects venom into its victims.*

Clamps and cutters *Ants' jaws, or mandibles, clamp down on prey and cut food into bite-size chunks.*

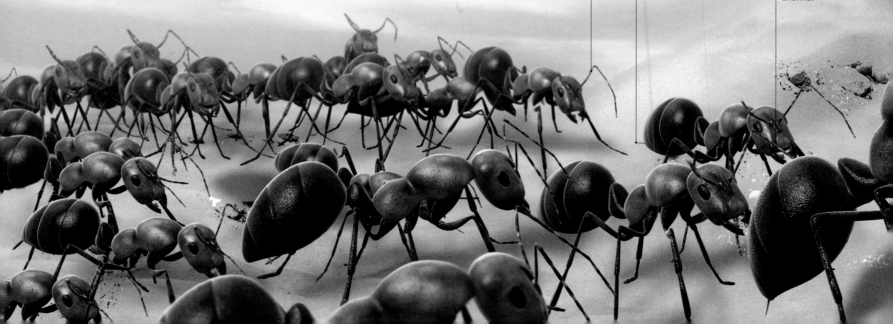

Inside *An ant's body is made up of three parts—the prosoma, or head; the mesosoma, in the middle; and the metasoma, at the end of the body.*

Prosoma
This is the head. It contains the brain.

Mesosoma
The legs attach to this area of the ant's body.

Metasoma
The abdomen holds the organs of breathing, blood circulation, and digestion.

Sting source
Venom is stored in a sac inside the ant's abdomen.

Hiding and
Traps

Generally, predators use one of two methods to catch prey. Some hunt actively, whereas others sit and wait for prey to come to them, then ambush it. Either way, hiding helps the predator. Active hunters may use stealth to get close to prey without being seen. Sit-and-wait predators use camouflaging colors or patterns to hide from approaching prey. Others, such as the amazing trapdoor spider, build camouflaged hideouts so that prey are unaware of the danger they are in until it is too late. This is just like some human hunters who build blinds among vegetation.

UNSEEN STALKERS

Camouflage allows predators to sneak up on prey or wait until the prey gets close to them. The element of surprise gives predators an advantage over the startled prey.

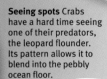

Eliminating shadows The Malaysian flying gecko has flaps on the edges of its body, which it flattens to stop a shadow from forming. Combined with coloring, this makes it virtually invisible to its prey.

Seeing spots Crabs have a hard time seeing one of their predators, the leopard flounder. Its pattern allows it to blend into the pebbly ocean floor.

White as snow The polar bear uses the color-matching technique of camouflage. Arctic snow hides its coat as it waits for a seal to surface.

A lion of larvae
Ant lions are insect larvae that dig pits. Ants and other insects fall in to be gobbled up by the ferocious predators that are buried below.

Time to eat An ant lion grasps an ant in its jaws and sucks up its fluids.

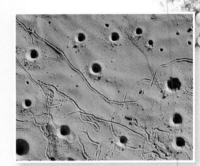

Pitfalls Small creatures should avoid the many ant lion pits found in dry, sandy soil.

1 **Spider hole cover**
A trapdoor spider caps its burrow with a hinged lid, hiding it from prey.

2 **Lying in wait**
When the spider senses an insect's vibrations, it pops open the lid to seize the prey.

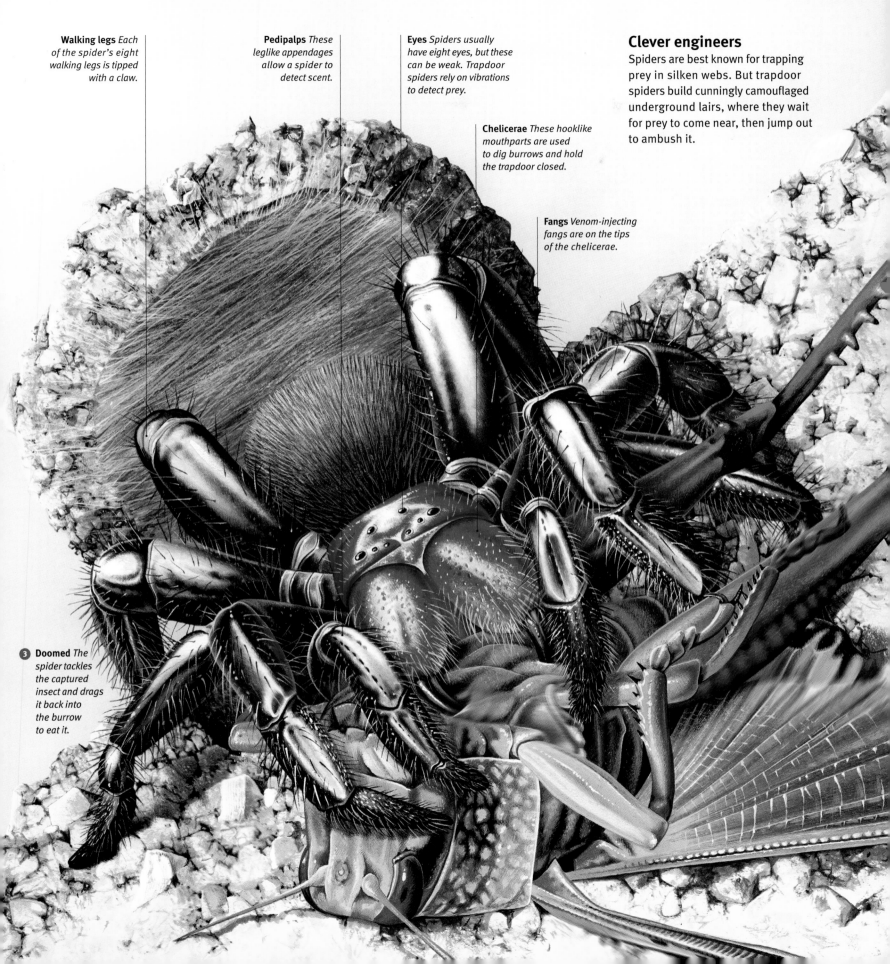

Walking legs *Each of the spider's eight walking legs is tipped with a claw.*

Pedipalps *These leglike appendages allow a spider to detect scent.*

Eyes *Spiders usually have eight eyes, but these can be weak. Trapdoor spiders rely on vibrations to detect prey.*

Chelicerae *These hooklike mouthparts are used to dig burrows and hold the trapdoor closed.*

Fangs *Venom-injecting fangs are on the tips of the chelicerae.*

Clever engineers

Spiders are best known for trapping prey in silken webs. But trapdoor spiders build cunningly camouflaged underground lairs, where they wait for prey to come near, then jump out to ambush it.

3 Doomed *The spider tackles the captured insect and drags it back into the burrow to eat it.*

Carnivorous
Plants

It is strange to think of plants as predators. Most plants make their own food by trapping the sunlight that fuels photosynthesis. But a few resilient plants have evolved to catch and digest small animals for food. Called carnivorous, or meat-eating, plants, they cannot move about like many animal predators do to find prey. Instead, their leaves are designed as clever lures to entice single-celled animals (called protozoa), insects, spiders, or even small frogs into their protein-digesting lairs.

Needing nitrogen

Carnivorous plants grow around the world in many different habitats, from rain forests to bogs and ponds. The soil in which they grow is usually low in nitrogen, which they get instead from the animals they consume.

No exit

Protozoa wander into a genlisea's, or corkscrew plant's, funnel-shaped underground trap through spiraling grooves. Inside, downward-pointing hairs keep the tiny animals from leaving and force them into the "stomach" of the plant.

False promise pitfall A brightly colored tropical pitcher plant lures insects with nectar droplets on the pitcher lips. As the insect feeds, it slips on the waxy pitcher wall and falls to its doom.

Genlisea

Armed flypaper *Insects landing on the sundew's tentacles are first stuck in drops of a sticky secretion, then held in place to be digested by the plant's enzymes.*

In the soup *Insects land in a bowl of digestive juices, where they are broken down and absorbed.*

Hair-trigger jaws

A Venus flytrap's two-part leaves, ringed with spiny teeth, snap shut like jaws when triggered by an insect touching the leaf's sensitive hairs.

1 The fly is lured with bright color and sweet secretions.

2 The fly touches the flytrap's sensitive hairs.

3 The trap snaps shut and the fly is slowly digested.

Underwater trap

Bladderworts have bladders with hair-covered trapdoors on their underwater stems. When a tiny aquatic animal touches the hairs, the trapdoor springs open, the animal is sucked into captivity, and the door closes behind it.

Killer
Senses

Human hunters rely on looking for and, to a lesser extent, listening for prey. Predatory birds and some mammals, such as cats, use vision and hearing too. Depending on the species, one of these senses may be better than the other for detecting prey. Bears, wolves, kiwi birds, and sharks generally sniff out their prey. Some snakes "hear" the vibrations of their moving prey, just as we can feel the vibration of the bass beat of a rock band. Sharks and other fish also sense vibrations, and some can detect the weak electrical currents coming from an animal's cells. But there are some animals that have uniquely specialized senses. The star-nosed mole "sees" with a super sense of touch. And many bats echolocate to detect objects as fine as a human hair.

A NOSE FOR AN EYE

Twenty-two finger-like pink appendages, or stars, ring a star-nosed mole's snout. Each is covered with thousands of touch receptors that feel prey in the mole's dark underground habitat.

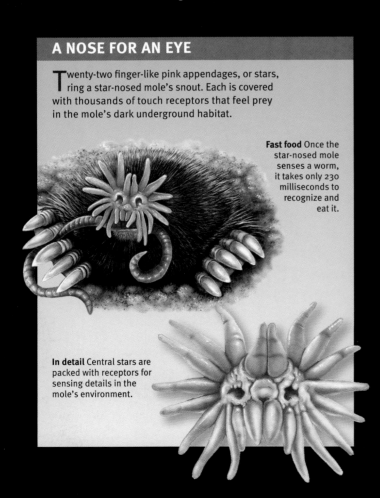

Fast food Once the star-nosed mole senses a worm, it takes only 230 milliseconds to recognize and eat it.

In detail Central stars are packed with receptors for sensing details in the mole's environment.

① Listening in the dark
Flying in the dark, a bat hunting a moth emits pulses of high-frequency sounds that are too high pitched for humans to hear.

④ Dinner is heard *As the bat homes in on the moth, the frequency of echoes increases until the bat embraces the moth in its wings and grabs it with its mouth.*

Under the skin
The snail-shaped hearing organs of a bat's inner ears, called cochleas, take up a large portion of its skull.

Cochlea

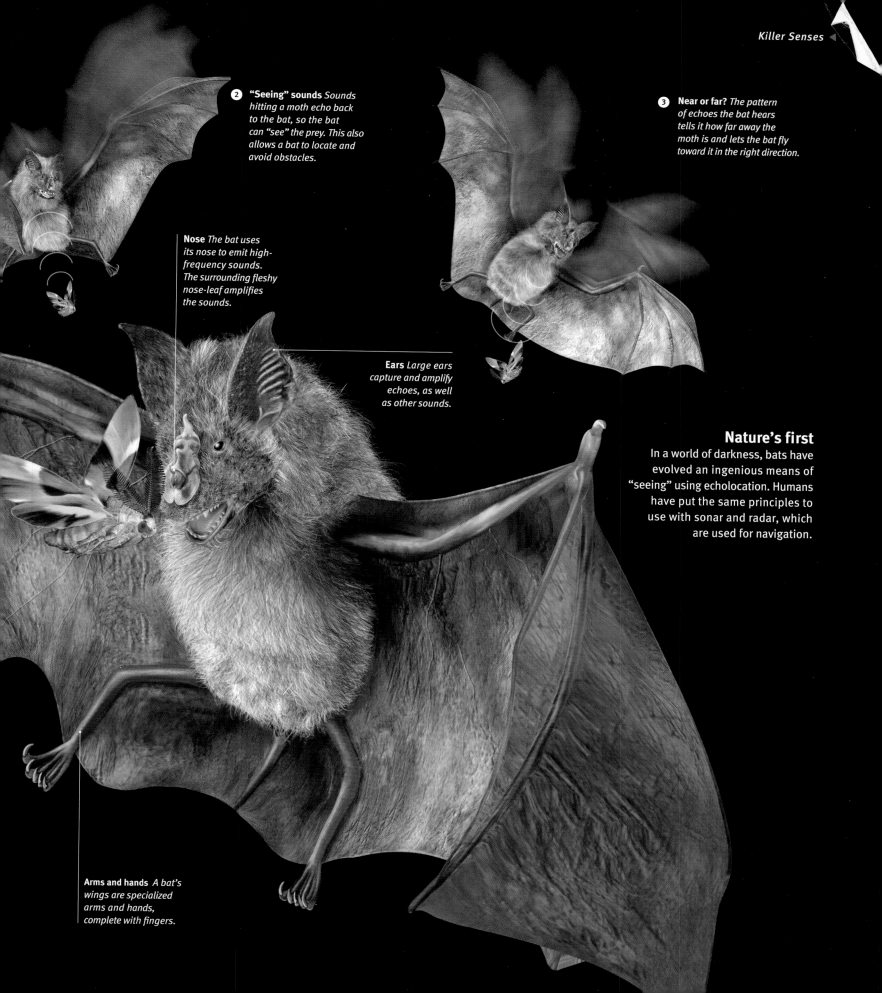

② **"Seeing" sounds** *Sounds hitting a moth echo back to the bat, so the bat can "see" the prey. This also allows a bat to locate and avoid obstacles.*

③ **Near or far?** *The pattern of echoes the bat hears tells it how far away the moth is and lets the bat fly toward it in the right direction.*

Nose *The bat uses its nose to emit high-frequency sounds. The surrounding fleshy nose-leaf amplifies the sounds.*

Ears *Large ears capture and amplify echoes, as well as other sounds.*

Nature's first
In a world of darkness, bats have evolved an ingenious means of "seeing" using echolocation. Humans have put the same principles to use with sonar and radar, which are used for navigation.

Arms and hands *A bat's wings are specialized arms and hands, complete with fingers.*

Creative
Killers

Most predators catch prey in much the same way: they search for it or wait for it to come their way. They then bite or sting, injecting venom or not, to kill the prey. But a few species have evolved unusual methods to attract or kill prey. Komodo dragons use the bacteria in their mouth to slowly kill prey that escapes after the dragon takes a bite. Desert death adders use a lure: buried in sand, they lift and wiggle their tail tip so they look like an insect larva—a tasty treat to birds and small mammals. When the duped prey gets near, it finds death instead of dinner.

Cookie cutting
Slow moving and only about 15 inches (38 cm) long, a cookie-cutter shark latches on to its prey using suction, then rotates its body, cutting a circular section of flesh from its victim.

Bright spark The cookie-cutter shark's underside glows, camouflaging it from fish swimming below. But a fish-shaped spot on its chin does not glow. This shadow attracts larger fish, which the shark can take a bite from when they come closer to investigate.

SHADOW HUNTING

Many predatory birds spread their wings over prey so others cannot swoop in. Black egrets use this same behavior to attract prey, which are lured by the appearance of safety the shadow creates.

1 Before the hunt Fish are wary and hard to catch in open waters.

2 No escape Thinking they have reached the safety of the riverbank, the fish gravitate to the shadow cast by the egret's wings. Once close, they make an easy target.

On the run
Komodos have strong legs for running and toes armed with sharp claws.

Long tail
The Komodo's long tail is used for balance when it runs to attack prey.

Death by germs

The Komodo dragon is the world's largest lizard. Agility and strong legs with clawed toes help it catch large prey. But the dragon's real trick is using fanglike teeth to inject deadly bacteria. When the prey dies from blood poisoning, the dragon follows its nose to find the rotting victim.

Potbelly *An expandable stomach lets a 300-pound (135-kg) dragon stuff in 240 pounds (110 kg) of meat in one meal.*

Terrible teeth *Curved, serrated teeth rip and tear the flesh of prey, as well as inject bacteria. Scientists have found about 50 kinds of bacteria in a Komodo dragon's saliva.*

Forked tongue *Its long, forked tongue can detect odors that help it find prey and carrion.*

SHARKS: THE FACTS

EXAMPLES: 500 species, including angel sharks, bullhead sharks, ground sharks, wobbegongs, and requiem sharks

TOOLS: Seven acute senses, teeth, strength

BIGGEST/SMALLEST: Whale shark/pygmy ribbontail catshark

PREY: Diverse sea animals and small plants (phytoplankton)

HUNTING METHODS: Search and pursuit, ambush, filter-feeding, searching the ocean floor

CONSERVATION STATUS: 100 species critically endangered to near-threatened

Fast facts Fast facts at your fingertips give you essential information about each predator group or habitat.

Locator map This map shows you where the featured predator group or habitat is located.

- Ocean locations
- Land and river locations

Classification bar This bar shows the classification of each predator group. This feature does not appear in the Predator Habitats section.

CATS: THE FACTS

EXAMPLES: 40 species of cats, including tigers, cheetahs, jaguarundis, ocelots, bobcats, lynx, and European wildcats

TOOLS: Teeth, claws, excellent vision, stealth, strength, speed

BIGGEST/SMALLEST: Tigers/rusty-spotted cats

PREY: Hoofed mammals, rabbits, rodents, birds

HUNTING METHODS: Ambush, stalk, chase

CONSERVATION STATUS: All except the domestic cat are of conservation concern

Hook in mouth

Tiny bumps with hooked tips, called papillae, cover a cat's tongue. They work like a rasp to scrape meat off bones.

Supreme Hunters

Cats

Cats are perfect predators. They have razor-sharp teeth set in powerful jaws, strong limbs ending in piercing claws, and agile, muscular bodies, all of which are designed for hunting. Cats are also pure carnivores, depending entirely on flesh to meet their nutritional needs. Tigers, lions, jaguars, leopards, snow leopards, and pumas hunt large prey, often animals larger than themselves. The smallest of these cats, the 100-pound (45-kg) puma, can single-handedly take down and kill an 800-pound (363-kg) bull elk. The largest, a 500-pound (227-kg) tiger, can capture a 2,000-pound (907-kg) wild cattle called a guar. These magnificent cats have only one major enemy: people.

1 **Off the box** *From a standing start, a lion accelerates like a sprinter to close the gap between it and its speedy prey.*

Camouflage coats
Beautiful fur coats keep cats warm. Their colors and patterns vary among species to help conceal the cats from prey in their diverse natural habitats.

Spots in the forest Coats with bold spots and blotches, like those of a jaguar, are typical of forest-living cats.

Disappearing act Black and orange stripes appear conspicuous to us but make a tiger disappear among tall grasses.

Snow suit The snow leopard's long, thick, pale fur is adapted to its cold, often snow-covered mountain habitat.

Black hides the spots Most leopards have spots on light background fur, but some have spots on black fur.

Going in for the kill

After a slow stalk, a lion bursts into a run to catch a gazelle. Using its strong front legs with clawed paws, the lion pulls the prey onto its side to keep its hooves at bay. Then the lion seizes the gazelle's throat to kill it.

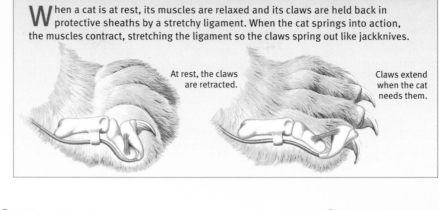

JACKKNIFE

When a cat is at rest, its muscles are relaxed and its claws are held back in protective sheaths by a stretchy ligament. When the cat springs into action, the muscles contract, stretching the ligament so the claws spring out like jackknives.

At rest, the claws are retracted.

Claws extend when the cat needs them.

2 Seizure *A lion seizes prey with its long, sharp claws and drags it to the ground.*

3 Two ways to kill *A lion kills either by biting a prey's throat until it suffocates or by seizing the nape of the prey's neck to crush its vertebrae.*

BEARS: THE FACTS

EXAMPLES:	Eight bear species, including polar, brown, American black, Asiatic black, sun, sloth, Andean, and giant panda
TOOLS:	Strength, teeth, claws, paws
BIGGEST/SMALLEST:	Polar bear/sun bear
PREY:	Great diversity among the species, from seals and elk to termites and plants
HUNTING METHODS:	Ambush, search and stalk, chase, steal other predators' kills
CONSERVATION STATUS:	Most species vulnerable or endangered

Towers of Strength

Bears

Bears are huge beasts, with burly bodies, long, sharp claws, and big heads with long canine teeth. They are carnivores, but only the immense polar bear feeds nearly exclusively on meat—that of ringed seals. Brown bears, sometimes called grizzlies, prey on moose and salmon, and eat carrion as well as roots, berries, insects, and honey. Smaller black bears hunt small mammals but eat mostly fruit and berries, while spectacled bears prefer fruit and nuts. Sloth bears specialize in ripping open ant and termite mounds to slurp up thousands of these tiny creatures. At the other extreme from polar bears, giant pandas eat only bamboo.

Knife, fork, and spoon
A bear's long, sharp claws (one of which is shown here at full size) can measure up to 4 inches (10 cm) long. They are a multifunctional tool for the bear, which uses them for cutting, ripping, slashing, spearing, holding, and digging.

No bones about it Long, heavy limb bones, robust shoulder bones, and a massive skull on a thick neck provide a framework for a polar bear's great strength.

BEARS: THE GREAT OMNIVORES

For almost every kind of food, there is a hungry bear species willing to eat it. This adaptable palate means that bears are often attracted to human foods, such as fruit and honey, and sometimes to our leftovers, which may lead them into conflict with people. Humans are a bear's only significant predator.

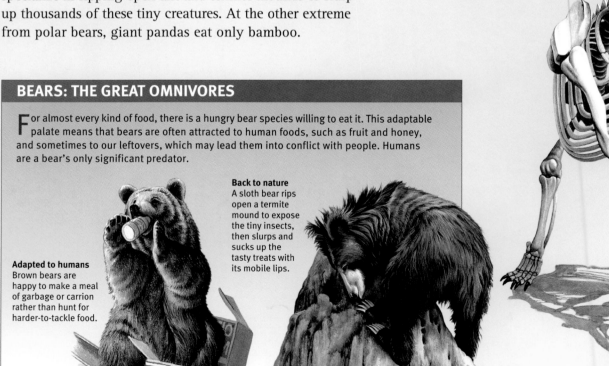

Adapted to humans
Brown bears are happy to make a meal of garbage or carrion rather than hunt for harder-to-tackle food.

Back to nature
A sloth bear rips open a termite mound to expose the tiny insects, then slurps up the tasty treats with its mobile lips.

Big, bad bear *Biggest of the bears, a male polar bear weighs in at up to 1,500 pounds (680 kg).*

Great white killer

Nearly invisible among the Arctic ice and snow, a polar bear waits for a seal to pop out of the ice for air, then kills and drags the victim out of the water with its powerfully clawed paws.

The nose knows *A strong sense of smell helps polar bears find the holes seals use to catch a breath.*

Teeth tools *A polar bear's sharp cheek teeth are used to shear meat off prey, and its long, sharp canines grab and hold prey.*

Paws rule *A polar bear's paws measure 12 inches (30 cm) across, the length of a standard ruler.*

MAMMALS

BIRDS

REPTILES AND AMPHIBIANS

FISH

INVERTEBRATES

WILD DOGS AND WOLVES: THE FACTS

EXAMPLES: 35 species of canids, including gray wolves, coyotes, African wild dogs, maned wolves, jackals, foxes

TOOLS: Excellent vision and sense of smell; teeth; sustained running; hunting in groups

BIGGEST/SMALLEST: Gray wolf/fennec fox

PREY: Hoofed mammals, rabbits and hares, rodents, birds, insects

HUNTING METHODS: Track and chase

CONSERVATION STATUS: All species are of conservation concern

Wild Dogs and

Wolves

On foot *Wolves are strong walkers and runners and stand on tiptoes on long, slim legs. They can run up to 40 miles per hour (64 km/h) for short distances.*

Wolves boast excellent vision and a fine sense of smell for finding and tracking prey; strong legs and lungs that enable them to pursue prey over long distances; and 42 deadly teeth in powerful jaws to rip apart prey. But the real predatory power of wolves and wild dogs comes from their hunting in packs. Working together, they can hunt and kill prey much larger than themselves. A 1,300-pound (590-kg) moose is no match for a pack of six or eight 100-pound (45-kg) wolves, and a 700-pound (315-kg) zebra is easily preyed upon by a pack of 10 to 20 African wild dogs, each weighing about 75 pounds (34 kg). However, some wild dogs, such as foxes, hunt alone or in pairs and prey on smaller animals such as rabbits and rodents.

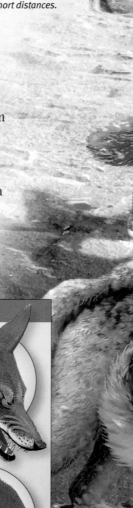

FACE OFF

The success of wild dogs is dependent on their ability to work as a team. To do this, they have complex methods of communication, including facial expressions, just like humans have. They also use sounds, scent marking, and body postures to communicate with other pack members.

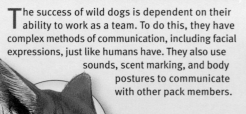

Friendly

Submissive

Attacking

Defending

Team effort

A pack of gray wolves may chase a moose for hundreds of yards until it slows down with exhaustion or is tripped up in deep snow. The wolves then move in for the kill. Each wolf bites a different part of the prey, from its nose, neck, and throat to its legs, flanks, and rump.

Leaders of the pack
A typical wolf pack is composed of an adult pair, their young pups, and older brothers and sisters. The adult male and female lead the pack.

Hearing it all *Wolves have excellent hearing, far better than that of a human. They can turn their large ears halfway around their heads to tell where a sound is coming from.*

MAMMALS

BIRDS

REPTILES AND AMPHIBIANS

FISH

INVERTEBRATES

SHARKS: THE FACTS

EXAMPLES: 500 species, including angel sharks, bullhead sharks, ground sharks, wobbegongs, and requiem sharks

TOOLS: Seven acute senses, teeth, strength

BIGGEST/SMALLEST: Whale shark/pygmy ribbontail catshark

PREY: Diverse sea animals and small plants (phytoplankton)

HUNTING METHODS: Search and pursuit, ambush, filter-feeding, searching the ocean floor

CONSERVATION STATUS: 100 species critically endangered to near-threatened

Kings of the Sea

Sharks

No word says "predator" better than "shark." A shark's huge mouthful of sharp, serrated teeth, designed to rip chunks of flesh off its victims, is coupled with a strong, lithe body that knifes through the water and lunges at prey with amazing speed. The largest sharks, such as the yacht-length whale shark, eat tiny marine plants and animals called plankton. About half of the 500 shark species are shorter than a yardstick and prey on small fish, shellfish, and clams. The serious shark predators are in the middle-size range—all are longer than the average adult man, and some, such as the great white, are three times as long. These sharks roam shallow coastal waters in search of prey such as seals and sea lions.

High-fat meal *Great white sharks hunt baby seals because half their body weight is fat.*

Lateral line *A shark's lateral line, which runs along the side of its body, detects movement and sound so the animal can turn toward the source.*

OCEAN DIVERSITY

Sharks have a wide range of tools and tricks to help them feed. These include sheer size, a wide head, or even an agile tail.

Sucking up
Opening its mouth very wide, a whale shark sucks up whole schools of zooplankton at a time.

Pin head
A hammerhead shark pins a stingray to the ocean floor with its wide head and bites off its wings.

Stunner
A thresher shark stuns fish by whacking them with its long tail fin.

Eyes *Sharks, and especially great whites, have excellent vision. They can see in color and in the dark.*

Chemical detector *A shark's sensitive nose can smell tiny amounts of odor chemicals, such as blood, in the water.*

Jaws on the loose
A shark's jaws are loosely connected to its skull, so it can push them out to make its gape wide enough to clamp down on large prey.

All in a row *Triangular serrated teeth grow in two or three rows, each with 26 teeth in the upper jaw and 24 in the lower.*

1 Here the shark's jaw is at rest, with jaws in a normal position.

2 Lifting the snout and pushing out the lower jaw widens the shark's gape.

3 Pushing out the upper jaw exposes the teeth. The shark is ready to bite.

Electricity in the water
Ampullae of Lorenzini, which are found on the shark's nose, are special pores that allow the shark to sense electrical impulses from potential prey.

Skin surface

Pore

Nerve cell

Feeding time
A great white shark, reaching 6,600 pounds (3,000 kg) in weight and 20 feet (6 m) in length, grabs a seal, sea lion, or dolphin in its toothy jaws and holds on until the prey gives up. When the blood drains out through its bite wounds, the prey floats to the water's surface and the shark swims in to eat it.

CROCODILES AND ALLIGATORS: THE FACTS

EXAMPLES: 23 species, including gharials, Chinese and American alligators, black caimans, and muggers

TOOLS: Strength, speed, stealth, sharp teeth, powerful jaws

BIGGEST/SMALLEST: Indopacific crocodile/dwarf caiman

PREY: Insects, frogs, reptiles, birds, mammals, fish

HUNTING METHODS: Ambush, using body and tail to herd prey

CONSERVATION STATUS: All species listed as being of conservation concern; four critically endangered

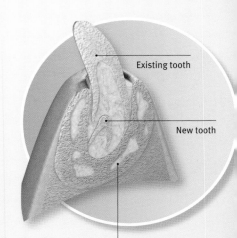

Existing tooth

New tooth

Trading teeth
Crocodiles and alligators replace their teeth regularly. A new tooth grows up and through the older one, whose crown then falls off.

Crocodiles and
Alligators

Crocodiles and alligators use strength, stealth, speed, and sharp teeth to feed their need for meat. Crocodiles, alligators, and their lesser-known relatives, caimans and gharials, range in size from the length of a bike to that of a limousine, but all are fierce predators. Exclusively carnivorous, these reptiles prey on any creature they can catch, from small fish to mammals as big as zebras. They can also eat unwary people. After a big meal, however, they may go for months without wanting another. Even then, the reptiles usually wait for food to come to them rather than waste energy on hunting.

SHAKE, RATTLE, AND ROLL

A crocodile shakes its prey until chunks break off. The chunks are swallowed whole. Stones in the crocodile's first stomach help to grind down the chunks, which are digested in the animal's highly acidic second stomach.

A saltwater crocodile shakes a kangaroo to break it apart.

Stones in the crocodile's stomach are called gastroliths.

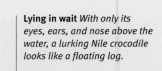

A tail up *With sweeps of its muscular tail, the crocodile powers through the water.*

Lying in wait *With only its eyes, ears, and nose above the water, a lurking Nile crocodile looks like a floating log.*

By a nose

Zebras can easily outrun a Nile crocodile on dry land, but they become sitting ducks when mired in the mud while drinking at a water hole. A Nile crocodile usually grabs its victim by its sensitive nose. The pain forces the zebra to let itself be dragged underwater, where the crocodile has the upper hand.

Jaw power *A crocodile's jaws snap shut with 3,000 pounds of pressure per square inch (200kg/cm²), five times stronger than a human jaw.*

Rocket croc *Blasting out of the water like a rocket, the crocodile creates havoc in a thirsty zebra herd and ensures one will be its victim.*

MAMMALS

BIRDS

REPTILES AND AMPHIBIANS

FISH

INVERTEBRATES

BIRDS OF PREY: THE FACTS

EXAMPLES: 500 species, including golden eagles, great horned owls, and red-tailed hawks

TOOLS: Sharp talons, good vision, sharp beak

BIGGEST/SMALLEST: Monkey-eating eagle/black-legged falconet

PREY: Monkeys, foxes, rodents, fish, other birds, insects

HUNTING METHODS: Stalking, soaring search, catching in talons

CONSERVATION STATUS: Most species vulnerable or endangered

Flying High

Birds of Prey

Excellent vision, powerful flight, strong feet ending in sharp, curved talons, and heavy, hooked beaks are the weapons of birds of prey. Birds of prey, including eagles, hawks, and owls, are often very large birds. A monkey-eating harpy eagle's wingspan is as wide as a professional basketball player is tall. Condors, which eat carrion, have wingspans as wide as a small airplane. Others are small and hunt insects or smaller birds. Not all predatory birds, however, are birds of prey, such as robins and crows. But any bird that hunts live prey for a living, rather than eating seeds or fruit, is a predator.

To catch a fish

From a high perch overlooking a pond or stream, this bald eagle spots a fish and swoops to grab it in its strong talons. The agile eagle then carries its treasure to the water's edge or a perch, where it rips off chunks of meat with its sharp beak.

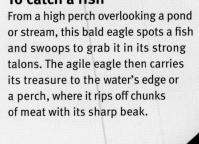

HUNTING IN STYLE

Predatory birds hunt in many ways, depending on the prey they hunt and where they catch it.

Bird bomb From a perch or high in the air, a falcon sights a bird and swoops—dropping like a laser-guided bomb to hit, stun, then snare the victim with its talons.

Diving for dinner
A kingfisher spies a fish from above the water. It hovers briefly while taking aim, then plunges into the water headfirst to snatch the fish in its heavy beak.

Kite flying A kite soars over woodlands, looking for dragonflies, cicadas, and other large insects. It then uses its talons to capture one of these morsels in midair.

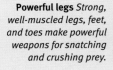

Powerful legs *Strong, well-muscled legs, feet, and toes make powerful weapons for snatching and crushing prey.*

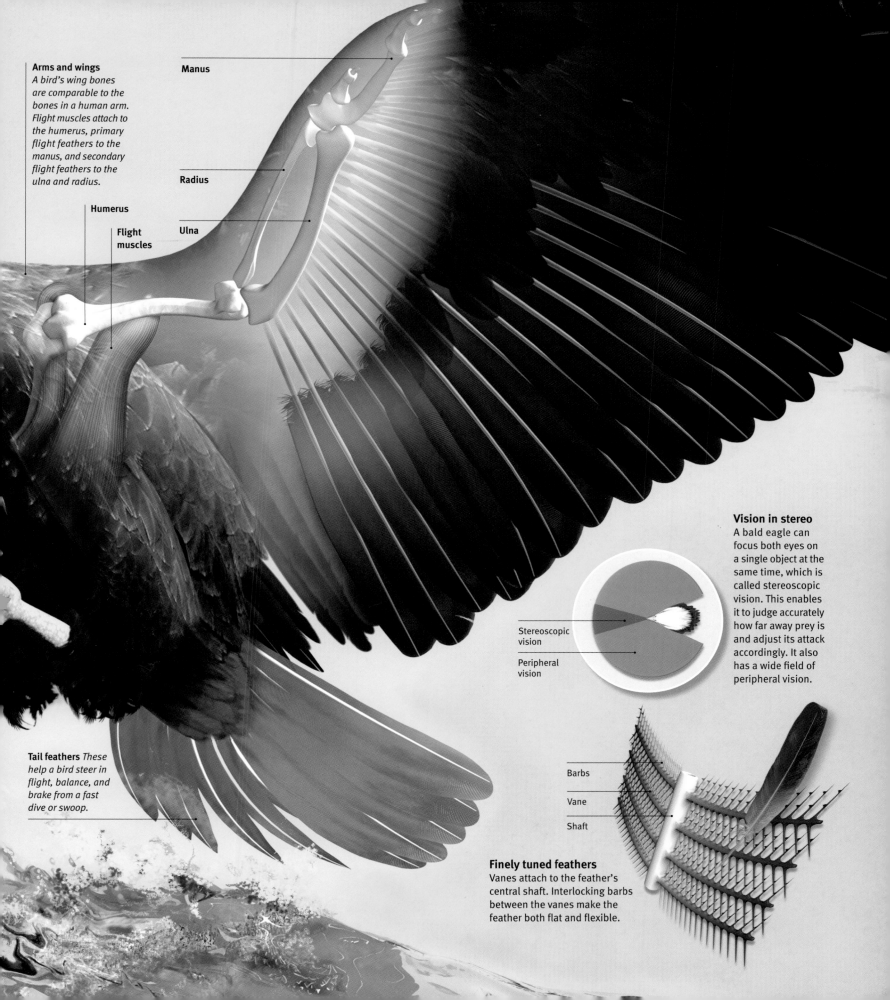

Arms and wings
A bird's wing bones are comparable to the bones in a human arm. Flight muscles attach to the humerus, primary flight feathers to the manus, and secondary flight feathers to the ulna and radius.

Manus

Radius

Humerus

Ulna

Flight muscles

Vision in stereo
A bald eagle can focus both eyes on a single object at the same time, which is called stereoscopic vision. This enables it to judge accurately how far away prey is and adjust its attack accordingly. It also has a wide field of peripheral vision.

Stereoscopic vision

Peripheral vision

Tail feathers *These help a bird steer in flight, balance, and brake from a fast dive or swoop.*

Barbs

Vane

Shaft

Finely tuned feathers
Vanes attach to the feather's central shaft. Interlocking barbs between the vanes make the feather both flat and flexible.

RAIN FORESTS: THE FACTS

LOCATION EXAMPLES: Amazon, central Africa, Southeast Asia, New Guinea, Australia, New Zealand

ANIMALS: Gorillas, orangutans, sloths, monkey-eating eagles, jaguars, tigers, tapirs, Sumatran and Javan rhinos

PLANTS: Strangler figs, palms, bamboos, orchids, bromeliads, lianas

THREATS: Fires, logging, palm oil plantations, agriculture, overhunting

Under the Canopy
Rain Forests

Tropical rain forests are found in parts of Africa, Asia, Australia, and South America, where more than 6 feet (1.8 m) of rain falls every year. More than two-thirds of all plant and animal species live in these habitats. The rain forests of these four continents are home to species that are different but have similar adaptations. Big cats, crocodiles, snakes, wild dogs, and birds of prey hunt in rain forests for hoofed mammals, rodents, birds, and other vertebrates. For example, tigers are top predators of deer and pigs in Asian rain forests; leopards prey on antelope and monkeys in African rain forests; and jaguars hunt turtles and peccaries in South America's Amazon—the world's largest rain forest. In Australia, the now-extinct Tasmanian tiger, a large carnivorous marsupial, may have preyed on plant-eating marsupials.

Taste of death
Some colorful poison dart frogs have enough toxins on their skin to kill any animal that tries to taste them. These frogs get their poison from the insects, spiders, and mites they hunt for food.

CLEVER EARS

Many carnivorous bats find food through echolocation, but frog-eating bats listen for male frogs' mating calls. When they hear the calls, the bats swoop down and use their their large canine teeth to pluck up the frogs.

A frog-eating bat can tell the size of a frog by its call.

Feeding frenzy
Most piranhas are omnivores that eat fruits and seeds as well as scales and flesh from fish and mammals. An injured animal's blood in shallow water attracts schools of piranhas that erupt into a feeding frenzy. The piranhas may strip the animal's carcass clean.

1 **Emerald tree boa** *With its head hanging toward the forest floor, an emerald tree boa waits for a small mammal to pass below. When one appears, the snake catches it with its long front fangs, pulls it closer, then coils its body tightly around it until the animal suffocates.*

2 **Meals big and rare** *Caimans lurk mostly submerged at the river's edge. They use their eyes, ears, and noses to scout for prey. Large caimans can tackle big mammals such as pigs and deer. After a feast like this, they may go for months before they eat again.*

3 **Turtle hunter** *With their sturdy canines and strong jaws, jaguars can crunch through the hard shells of aquatic turtles, which they hunt at the water's edge. Jaguars are the only cats that regularly eat turtles.*

River of no return

Under a canopy of tangled vegetation, a slow-moving river in South America's Amazon rain forest looks peaceful. But in and around the river, danger lurks. Jaguars catch and crunch on turtles; camouflaged caimans and emerald tree boas wait for prey to come to them; and fierce piranhas are always ready to bite.

The Heat of the Sun

Deserts

Deserts cover about one-fourth of the land on Earth and are found on every continent. Some are hot and dry, such as Africa's Sahara. Others, like the Gobi in Asia, are hot in summer and cold in winter. Polar regions are also considered deserts. Deserts receive less than 10 inches (25 cm) of rain every year, but years may go by with no rain at all. Temperatures in deserts can reach more than 120°F (49°C) during the day or in summer and plunge to -40°F (-40°C) at night or in winter. Despite this, deserts host a diversity of plants, predators, and prey that survive on little or no water and tolerate extreme temperatures. Some top desert predators and their prey are cheetahs and gazelles in Africa, golden eagles and jackrabbits in North America, and wolves and wild asses in Asia.

FAST RUNNER

Roadrunners race along the desert surface at speeds of up to 15 miles per hour (24 km/h) to catch prey. At nearly 2 feet (0.6 m) tall, they are big enough and fast enough to run down snakes, lizards, small rodents, birds, and insects.

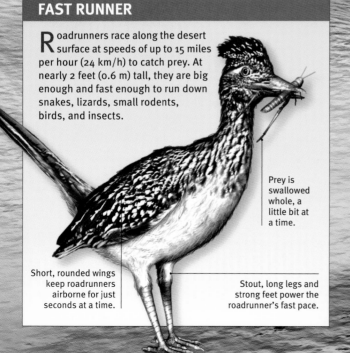

Prey is swallowed whole, a little bit at a time.

Short, rounded wings keep roadrunners airborne for just seconds at a time.

Stout, long legs and strong feet power the roadrunner's fast pace.

Desert monster *The Gila monster is one of only two venomous lizards. It chews its toxic saliva into the flesh of young rabbits, small rodents, and birds. Once the monster bites, it hangs on until its slow-acting venom kills its prey.*

Giant vulture *Soaring above the desert, turkey vultures with 6-foot (2-m) wingspans search for meals of carrion. Unlike most birds, turkey vultures have a keen sense of smell, which they use to track down the stench of rotting flesh.*

Giant stinger *At 6 inches (15 cm) long, the giant desert hairy scorpion is the largest in North America. It catches and holds small prey in its strong pincers, then flips its tail around to sting prey by injecting its deadly venom.*

Heat-seeking missile *Also called the horned rattlesnake, the sidewinder moves quickly along the sandy desert surface, swinging its body from side to side. It chases mice, rats, and lizards by detecting the body heat of its prey.*

Late in the day

In the hot Sonoran Desert of the southwestern United States, many predators hunt prey at dawn or dusk, when it is cooler than the heat of day. Sidewinders home in on small rodents. Gila monsters grab rabbits that are nibbling small plants, and stinging scorpions go after blind snakes.

POLAR: THE FACTS

LOCATION EXAMPLES: Bering Sea, Antarctic Peninsula, Weddell Sea

ANIMALS: Polar bears, seals, whales, penguins, krill, squid, wingless midges

PLANTS: Plankton, mosses, sedges, grasses

THREATS: Global climate change, oil and gas drilling, mining, overfishing, overhunting

Above and Below the Ice
Polar

A surprising number of cold-hardy animals make their homes near the North and South poles of the Arctic and Antarctic. Seals, kept warm by thick layers of blubber, live at both poles, alongside orcas, sperm whales, and skuas. Polar bears live only in the Arctic, and penguins inhabit only the Antarctic. But the most important animals in both areas are the krill that live in the icy waters. Krill form the basis of polar food webs. If a polar predator does not eat krill, it almost certainly eats animals that do. Krill themselves eat phytoplankton, tiny, free-floating plants; as well as zooplankton, tiny, free-floating animals. Scientists estimate that in the Antarctic alone, there are hundreds of millions of tons of krill.

Egg thief *Although skuas eat mostly fish, eggs snatched from penguins' nests make a tasty treat during the breeding season.*

Chilling out in Antarctica

Frigid air temperatures and icy waters do not slow down the polar predators of Antarctica. Here, even large predators become prey, and minute krill eat even tinier animals. Squid hunt fish, and penguins hunt squid and fish. Both squid and penguins are hunted by orcas. Skuas eat penguin eggs—and one another!

SIEVE MOUTH

The crabeater seal, which eats krill not crabs, has remarkable teeth. Each tooth has several gaps. When the upper and lower jaws come together, the holes create a sieve. After the seal closes its mouth around a krill swarm, the gaps strain out the water and keep the krill inside.

Krill

The tooth parts that create the sieve are called tubercules.

Top of the food chain *Mighty orcas, or killer whales, are the Antarctic's supreme predators. Penguins, squid, seals, and even other whales are no match for an orca.*

Crashing crabeaters *Millions of crabeater seals live on the ice and in the waters of Antarctica, where they feed on krill. However, global climate change is causing krill numbers to decline, and seal numbers may follow.*

Eat and be eaten *Krill live in dense swarms, so predators that hit on a swarm go into a feeding frenzy. Krill themselves dine on algae, tiny marine plants called phytoplankton, and tiny marine animals called zooplankton.*

King penguins *These speedy swimmers pursue small fish and squid. They use their flippers to fly through the icy water and dive as deep as 1,000 feet (300 m). However, while foraging, they risk becoming meals for orcas and leopard seals.*

Favorite food *Squid are abundant in Antarctic waters. Scientists estimate that these waters support 100 million tons (90 million t) of squid— and whales, seals, and seabirds eat about one third of them each year.*

Under the Sea
Coral Reefs

Coral reefs are amazing underwater structures, part living and part dead. They are made of the limestone skeletons of coral polyps—living animals—left behind when the polyps die. It takes thousands of years for a reef to form. The world's largest, the Great Barrier Reef, off the east coast of Australia, started to form about 20,000 years ago. Found only in fairly shallow tropical waters, most of the world's reef areas are in the Indian and Pacific oceans, with a few in the Atlantic and Caribbean. Coral reefs cover only a tiny part of the ocean bottom but support the most diverse and colorful set of animals found anywhere in the sea. The predators that haunt coral reefs range from huge sharks to flower-like sea anemones.

Sand maker *Parrot fish's front teeth are fused to form a beak used to chew coral and extract the algae. The ground-up coral is excreted as sand—up to a ton (0.9 t) per fish per year.*

Vacuum *A grouper lies in wait for a fish to swim nearby, then quickly puffs up its gill covers to create a vacuum action that sucks the prey into its mouth.*

Blue-ringed octopus *The most venomous of any sea creature, this octopus's bite paralyzes prey within seconds. It uses its beak to rip off and eat soft body parts.*

Algae eaters *Corals get most of their energy from algae called zooxanthellae, which live in the coral polyps. They also eat tiny marine animals called zooplankton, which they catch in their long, stinging tentacles.*

Harpooned *A cone shell fires its venom-packed barbed radula from its mouth to spear a small fish, then pulls the radula and the fish back into its mouth to eat it.*

CORAL KILLER

Crown-of-thorns sea stars are voracious predators of coral. Previously their numbers have been kept in check by the giant triton sea snail: their main predator. Unfortunately, humans have begun to harvest the giant triton, and the sea stars have grown in numbers. This has resulted in major destruction of the reef.

Giant triton devouring a crown-of-thorns sea star

Wet and weird

Australia's Great Barrier Reef is home to an assortment of weird predators wielding different tools to find and catch prey. Dainty-looking cone shells unleash harpoons; hefty groupers vacuum up prey; huge triggerfish use chisels; and hammerhead sharks constantly surf the reef for prey.

Bait and strike *In the blink of an eye, a reef cuttlefish can strike a small fish with tentacles full of paralyzing venom.*

Power tool *The very broad head of hammerhead sharks means these predators can easily scan wide expanses of ocean, searching for the electrical signals of prey.*

Titan triggerfish *This fish uses its chisel-like teeth and powerful jaws to crunch coral, shellfish, and spiny sea urchins.*

Flower power *When a fish or crustacean brushes against the petal-like tentacles of the sea anemone, it shoots out a venom-filled harpoon to capture and kill its prey.*

Ocean cleaner *Crabs are not fussy eaters and will eat almost anything, including crustaceans, algae, and ocean debris.*

Fast food *Thompson's gazelles are faster than every other Serengeti animal except the cheetah. Unfortunately, this gazelle is one of the cheetah's favorite foods.*

Across the Plains

Grasslands

Savannas, pampas, plains, steppes, and the outback are all grasslands. There is not enough rain each year for many trees to grow, but seasonal rains stimulate a rapid growth of grasses that many herbivores feast on. Carnivores then feast on these herbivores. Wolves hunt grass-eating bison in the North American plains. Golden eagles prey on saiga antelope in the Eurasian steppe, and puma prey on guanacos in South America's pampas. In the Australian outback, dingoes feed on kangaroos. In the African savanna, lions pursue wildebeest and zebras. Because rain does not fall on all parts of a grassland at the same time, many plant eaters migrate long distances to find vegetation. Their predators follow along.

Drinking dangerously *With water in short supply on the plains, wildebeest must gather at small water holes to drink, despite the deadly crocodiles that lurk there.*

① **First to feast** After killing a zebra, lions keep all other competitors, such as hyenas and vultures, at bay until they have eaten their fill.

③ **Cleaning up** Vultures often join feeding hyenas and sometimes beat them to the lions' leftovers. They poke their heads into the parts of a carcass mammals cannot reach, and use their beaks to tear the last scraps of meat off bones.

Perilous plains

A host of predators, including cunning leopards and ferocious crocodiles, stalk the Serengeti plains of eastern Africa. Their prey, mostly hoofed mammals such as wildebeest and warthogs, are constantly on the alert for signs of danger but still fall victim to the hunters. Water holes are particularly unsafe places.

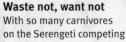

Waste not, want not
With so many carnivores on the Serengeti competing for meat, no part of a kill is wasted, and few predators will turn down food killed by another predator.

② **Next in line** When lions abandon a kill, hyenas close in to eat any leftover meat. Unlike lions, they can crack open bones to get at the juicy marrow inside.

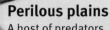

Swift kicker *With hooves as big as dinner plates, an adult giraffe can kill a lion with a swift kick, so predators mostly ignore these tall giants.*

Antitheft device *A leopard hauls its warthog prey up a tree so lions, wild dogs, and hyenas, which do not climb, cannot steal it.*

Water bound *The Nile crocodile's eyes and nostrils are on the top of its head so that it can float undetected toward prey.*

DECOMPOSER

Dung beetles are found in terrestrial habitats around the world. They eat the feces of mammals, such as zebras and wildebeest. By breaking it down, the beetles return the nutrients found in the dung back to the soil.

Rolling in it Dung beetles roll dung into balls by pushing it along the ground. This helps them transport it.

Diverse Predators

Classifying predators

The animal kingdom is sorted into groups based on how closely they are related to one another. This provides a way of organizing everything we know and discover about predators and prey.

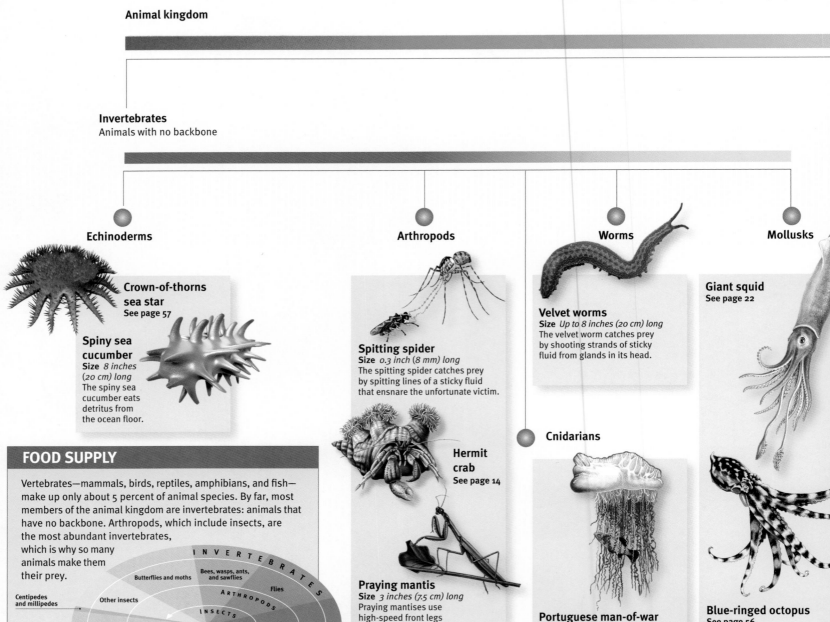

Animal kingdom

Invertebrates
Animals with no backbone

Echinoderms

Arthropods

Worms

Mollusks

Cnidarians

Crown-of-thorns sea star
See page 57

Spiny sea cucumber
Size *8 inches (20 cm) long*
The spiny sea cucumber eats detritus from the ocean floor.

Spitting spider
Size *0.3 inch (8 mm) long*
The spitting spider catches prey by spitting lines of a sticky fluid that ensnare the unfortunate victim.

Hermit crab
See page 14

Praying mantis
Size *3 inches (7.5 cm) long*
Praying mantises use high-speed front legs to snatch prey.

Ichneumon wasps
Size *Up to 5 inches (12.5 cm) long*
These wasps lay their eggs in the bodies of other insects. When the eggs hatch, the young eat the doomed host.

Velvet worms
Size *Up to 8 inches (20 cm) long*
The velvet worm catches prey by shooting strands of sticky fluid from glands in its head.

Giant squid
See page 22

Portuguese man-of-war
See page 21

Sea anemone
See page 57

Blue-ringed octopus
See page 56

Nudibranches
Size *Up to 23 inches (57.5 cm) long*
Nudibranches, or sea slugs, feed on other ocean invertebrates. Some also eat other nudibranches.

FOOD SUPPLY

Vertebrates—mammals, birds, reptiles, amphibians, and fish—make up only about 5 percent of animal species. By far, most members of the animal kingdom are invertebrates: animals that have no backbone. Arthropods, which include insects, are the most abundant invertebrates, which is why so many animals make them their prey.

INVERTEBRATES

Butterflies and moths

Bees, wasps, ants, and sawflies

ARTHROPODS

Flies

Other insects

INSECTS

Centipedes and millipedes

Arachnids

Beetles

Crustaceans

Mollusks

Fish
Amphibians
Reptiles
Birds
Mammals

VERTEBRATES

Segmented worms
Cnidarians
Roundworms
Flatworms
Other invertebrates

Small

Despite its small size—as small as 0.5 inch (1 cm)—krill is the main food source for the blue whale, the largest predator on Earth. Krill prey on phytoplankton.

Large

The blue whale is the largest predator in the world. Its tongue alone is as large as an elephant. It measures 110 feet (34 meters) in length.

Vertebrates

Animals with a backbone

Fish

Amphibians

Reptiles

Birds

Mammals

Stonefish
See page 21

Poison dart frog
See page 15

Komodo dragon
See pages 34–35

Albatross
Size *Wingspan of up to 11 feet (3.4 m)*
These large birds feed on squid, fish, and krill.

Snow leopard
See page 38

Gulper eel
Size *Up to 6.5 feet (2 m) long*
A gulper eel uses its mouth like a net by opening it wide and swimming at its prey.

Fire salamander
Size *Up to 12 inches (30 cm) long*
Fire salamanders eat mostly invertebrates. They have a special sticky tongue that prey, once caught, cannot escape from.

Snail-eating turtle
Size *Up to 7.8 inches (20 cm) long*
This Malaysian turtle lives in water, where it preys on snails and other invertebrates.

Secretary bird
Size *Up to 4 feet (1.2 m) tall*
The unusual secretary bird hunts prey on foot. It preys on mammals, lizards, snakes, and carrion.

Weasel
Size *Up to 14 inches (35 cm) long*
Weasels, though small, are ferocious predators that feed on other small mammals.

Sailfish
See page 24

Congo eel
Size *Up to 3.2 feet (1 m) long*
The Congo eel preys on frogs, snakes, fish, crustaceans, insects, and even other Congo eels.

Fire-bellied toad
Size *Up to 2.7 inches (7 cm) long*
The fire-bellied toad scares away predators by exposing its brightly colored underside.

Coral pipe snake
Size *Average 24 inches (60 cm) long*
The coral pipe snake is highly poisonous and preys on other snakes as well as lizards and small rodents.

King penguin
See page 55

Dolphin
See page 26

Shortfin mako shark
Size *Up to 13 feet (4 m) long*
This speedy shark is known for its aggressive behavior and ability to jump out of the water.

Flamingo
See page 16

Brown bear
See page 40

Glossary

adaptations A set of features—anatomical structures as well as behaviors—that enable animals to survive and reproduce successfully in the habitats in which they live.

ambush To lie in wait for prey to approach, then attack.

amphibian Vertebrate animals that can live on land and in water. Frogs, salamanders, toads, and newts are amphibians.

ampullae Sensory cells connected to nerves; found in sharks.

antennae Sensitive feelers on an insect's head.

arboreal Living in trees; adapted to life in trees.

bacteria Single-celled microorganisms (tiny life forms). Some bacteria cause infections; others are useful.

beak The sharp bill of a bird. In birds of prey the beak is hooked and is used to spear, carry, and tear apart prey.

binocular vision The ability to focus both eyes at once on an object. This enables predators to accurately determine the distance to prey.

bioluminescence The creation of light by living organisms, such as the cookie-cutter shark.

biome A major group of distinctive plant and animal communities adapted to a large region's natural environment. Tropical rain forest is one example of a biome.

birds of prey Flesh-eating birds such as hawks, eagles, and owls.

camouflage The way an animal blends into its environment in order to sneak up on prey or hide from predators.

canid A member of the family Canidae, which includes dogs, wolves, and foxes.

canine teeth The teeth between the front incisor teeth and the side molars. Cats use their long, sharp canine teeth to kill prey.

carnassials Scissor-like molar teeth that predators use to tear chunks of meat from a carcass.

carnivore An animal that eats meat.

chelicerae Pincer-like biting mouthparts found in spiders, scorpions, ticks, and mites.

claws Sharp, curved nails on the toes of animals, which are used to catch prey, dig, and climb.

climate change See *global climate change*.

colony A group of animals of the same species that live, hunt, and defend themselves together.

competitors Two or more animals that fight for the same food, territory, or mating partners.

conservation The effort to maintain Earth's natural resources, including wildlife, for future generations.

desert A dry region receiving less than 10 inches (25 cm) of rain annually.

diurnal Active during the day.

echolocation A way to detect prey by emitting sounds and listening for their echo from objects in the environment. Many bat species use echolocation to find prey.

endangered species Species that are likely to die out (become extinct) unless people take action to protect them.

extinct No longer living. When the last living member of a species dies, the species is extinct.

fangs Long, hollow teeth in snakes and spiders that pierce flesh and inject venom.

fish A group of vertebrate animals adapted to life in water, with gills for breathing.

food pyramid See *trophic pyramid*.

gastroliths Stones that some animals, such as crocodiles, swallow and use to help grind up food in their digestive tract.

gills Organs in fish that allow them to breathe underwater; comparable to lungs.

global climate change Usually refers to rapid, human-caused changes in climate, especially increasing temperatures around the world.

habitat The place where an animal lives in the wild, such as forest or grassland. An animal's habitat provides the right environment for survival and contains food, water, shelter, and potential mates.

herbivore An animal that eats primarily plant material. Many of the species that cats prey on, such as deer, antelope, and rabbits, are herbivores.

hooves The toes of horses, deer, antelope, and related animals, which are covered in thick, hard skin with sharp edges.

incisor teeth The front teeth of mammals. Cats use their incisor teeth for fine work such as plucking feathers from a bird carcass.

insects A large group of small invertebrates, such as flies, bees, and ants. Insects have three-part bodies, six legs, and usually two pairs of wings.

invertebrates Animals without backbones, such as insects, spiders, octopuses, jellyfish, and many others.

lateral line A series of sensory pores along the head and sides of fish and sharks used to detect water currents, vibrations, and pressure changes.

ligament Thick tissue that connects two bones.

mammal A group of vertebrates that feeds its young with milk. Cats, dogs, rats, monkeys, deer, whales, people, and other creatures with fur or hair are mammals.

mandibles The biting jaws of an insect.

marine Living in the ocean.

molars The flat teeth of a mammal found toward the back of the mouth, used for grinding food.

nitrogen Chemical element essential for the growth of plants and animals.

nocturnal Active at night.

nutrients Chemical compounds in food, such as proteins and fats, that enable animals to function and grow.

olfaction The sense of smell.

pack A group of animals of the same species that hunt together. Many canids form packs.

pampa The word used in South America for grassland.

pedipalps A specialized part of scorpions used as pincers.

plankton Tiny, free-floating marine plants, called phytoplankton, and animals, called zooplankton.

poaching Hunting animals illegally.

poison A substance that causes illness or death when touched or eaten, sometimes even in very small amounts.

predator An animal that hunts, kills, and eats other animals to survive.

prey Animals that are hunted, killed, and eaten by other animals called predators.

pride A group of female lions and their young. The females in a pride are usually related. Males attach themselves to prides of females.

quills Long, sharp hairs found on porcupines, echidnas, and a few other mammals.

rain forest A forest that receives at least 100 inches (about 250 cm) of rainfall annually. Most rain forests are in tropical regions of the world.

raptors Birds of prey.

reptiles A group of vertebrate animals with dry, scaly skin, including lizards, snakes, turtles, and crocodiles.

rodent A group of animals that includes rats and mice. Rodents are the primary prey of many predatory mammals and birds.

savanna An area with relatively sparse mixed vegetation of grasses, trees, and shrubs.

scavenger An animal that eats meat killed by other predators.

sharks A group of vertebrate animals that lives in water. The skeletons of sharks are made of cartilage whereas other fish skeletons are made of bone.

species A group of animals with very similar features. Individual members of a species are able to breed and produce live young that are fertile (able to breed when they, too, become adults). Under natural conditions, individuals of different species do not interbreed, but some exceptions occur. The species is the basic unit in scientific classification of animals and plants.

spiders A group of small invertebrates with eight legs.

spines Long, sharp structures that can pierce flesh and sometimes inject venom.

steppe A type of grassland found in northern Eurasia.

stingers Hollow structures on the tails and heads of insects and the tails of scorpions that pierce flesh and inject venom and saliva.

talons The long, curved nails on the feet of birds of prey.

tentacles Long, thin, moving structures on marine invertebrates that are used to feel, grasp, and inject venom.

terrestrial Living on land; adapted to living on land.

territory A home range that an animal or group of animals of the same species lives in and defends from other members of its species, especially those of the same sex.

trophic pyramid A graphical representation used to show that meat-eating predators, at the top of the food chain, are more rare than plant-eating animals, which, in turn, are less abundant than plants.

ungulates Large, plant-eating mammals with hooves. They include elephants, rhinoceroses, horses, deer, antelopes, wild cattle, and their relatives.

venom Poison that is injected by animals into a predator or prey through fangs, stingers, spines, and similar structures. Antivenin is medicine used to treat people who have been bitten by venomous animals.

vertebrae The bones that make up the spines, or backbones, of vertebrates.

vertebrates Animals with backbones. They include fish, sharks, amphibians, reptiles, birds, and mammals.

Index

A

African wild dogs, 26
albatross, 61
alligators, 46–7
anacondas, 22–3
ant lions, 28
antennae, 26
ants, 26–7
Argentinosaurus, 10
aye-aye, 18

B

bacteria, injecting prey with, 34–5
bald eagles, 48–9
bats, 32–3, 50
beaks, 16, 18, 48
bears, 18, 32, 40–1
birds of prey, 48–9, 50
bison, 13, 58
biting, 14, 20, 39, 43, 56
black bears, 40
black egrets, 34
bladderworts, 31
blue-ringed octopuses, 56
Brazilian wandering spiders, 21
brown bears, 40

C

caiman, 46, 51
camouflage, 15, 28, 34, 38, 46
carnivorous plants, 30–1
cats, 38–9, 50
cheetahs, 24–5, 52, 58
claws, 11, 18, 29, 38, 39, 40
cod, 13
colobus monkey, 13
coloration, 15, 38
condors, 48
cone shells, 56, 57
congo eel, 61
cookie-cutter shark, 34
coral pipe snake, 61
coral reefs, 56–7
corkscrew plant, 30
crabeater seals, 55
crocodiles, 22, 46–7, 50, 59
crown of thorns starfish, 57
Cynognathus, 10

D

desert death adders, 34
deserts, 52–3
dinosaurs, 10–11
dodos, 12
dolphins, 26
dung beetles, 59

E

eagles, 9, 48
ears, 32, 33, 43
echidnas, 15
echolocation, 32–3, 50
Egyptian cobra, 21
emerald tree boa, 50, 51
eyes, 18, 23, 29, 45

F

falcons, 48
fangs, 20–1, 29
feathers, 18, 49
feet, 19, 48
fire salamander, 61
flamingo, 16
food chain, 8

G

gastroliths, 46
gharials, 46
giant desert hairy scorpion, 53
giant squid, 22
giant tortoise, 12
giant triton, 57
Giganotosaurus, 10
Gila monster, 52, 53
giraffes, 59
golden eagles, 52, 58
grass snake, 9
grasslands, 58–9
great auk, 12
great white shark, 44
groupers, 56, 57
gulper eel, 61

H

Haast's giant eagles, 12
habitats, 30, 38, 50–9
hairs, 30–1
hammerhead sharks, 44, 57
hawks, 16, 48
hearing, 32, 43
hermit crabs, 14
hooves, 59
horns, 14
hunting, 10
    groups and packs, in, 26–7
    shadow hunting, 34
    styles of birds of prey, 48
hyenas, 22, 58, 59

I

ichneumon wasp, 60

J

jaguars, 38, 50, 51
jaws, 10, 17, 22, 23, 26, 28, 31, 38, 42, 45, 47, 51, 55

K

killer whales, 54, 55
king penguins, 55
kingfishers, 48
kites, 48
Komodo dragons, 34–5

L

leaf-cutter ant soldiers, 14
leafy sea dragons, 15
legs, 19, 29, 42, 48
leopard flounder, 28
leopards, 38, 50, 59
lions, 8, 38–9, 58, 59
lizards, 9
    venomous, 34–5, 52
lobster, 18

M

Malaysian flying gecko, 28
mantis shrimp, 25
moas, 12
Moray eels, 26
musk oxen, 14

N

Nile crocodile, 46–7, 59
nitrogen, 30
noses, 33, 41, 45
nostrils, 23
nudibranch, 60

O

ocean food pyramid, 8
orcas, 54, 55
owls, 18–19, 48
oxpeckers, 14

P

pack hunters, 10
pack leaders, 43
parrotfish, 56
passenger pigeons, 12
paws, 41
penguins, 54
peregrine falcon, 24–5

pincers, 53
piranhas, 50
pitcher plant, 30
poison dart frogs, 15, 20, 51
poisons, 15
polar bears, 28, 40–1, 54
polar regions, 54–5
polyphemus silkmoth, 15
Portuguese man-of-war, 21
praying mantis, 60
predators
    extinct, 10–11
    fastest, 24–5
    humans as, 12–13, 38, 40
    largest, 10
    methods of killing, 34–5
    plants, 30–1
    size, 22–3, 35, 41
    teamwork, 26–7, 42
prey
    defenses, 14–15
    evolution, 14
pterosaurs, 10
pumas, 9, 38

R

rain forest habitat, 50–1
reef cuttlefish, 57
roadrunners, 52

S

sailfish, 24
scent marking, 42
scorpions, 20, 53
sea anemones, 56, 57
seals, 28, 41, 54, 55
secretary bird, 61
senses, 32–3
shadow hunting, 34
sharks, 8, 16, 32, 44–5, 56, 61
shells, 14
shortfin mako shark, 61
shrimp, 8, 25
sidewinders, 53
size, 22–3, 35, 41
skuas, 54, 55
skulls, 11, 17, 32
sloth bears, 40
smell, sense of, 52
snail-eating turtle, 61
snakes, 9, 20–1, 22–3, 32, 50, 52, 53, 61
sniffing out prey, 11, 32
snow leopards, 38
sounds, 32, 42
speed, 24–5, 44, 46, 52
    acceleration, 24, 38

sperm whales, 22, 54
spiders, 28–9, 60
spines, 15
spiny sea cucumber, 60
spitting spider, 60
squid, 55
star-nosed mole, 32
stick insects, 15
stingers, 20, 26, 27
stonefish, 21
strength, 22–3, 40, 46, 47
sundew plant, 31

T

tails, 10, 34, 46, 53
talons, 18–19, 48
teamwork, 26–7, 42
teeth, 10, 11, 16–17, 21, 22, 35, 38, 41, 42, 44–5, 46, 55
tentacles, 21, 57
terns, 16
Thompson's gazelle, 58
thresher sharks, 44
tigers, 13, 16–17, 38, 50
Titan triggerfish, 57
toes, 19
tongues, 16, 35, 38
trap-jaw ant, 25
trapdoor spiders, 28–9
traps, 28–9, 30
turkey vultures, 52
Tyrannosaurus, 10

V

velvet worm, 60
venom, 20–1, 26, 27, 53, 56
Venus flytrap, 31
vibrations, 29, 32
vision, 32, 48
    stereoscopic, 49
vultures, 58

W

wasp beetles, 15
weasel, 61
webs, 29
whale sharks, 44
wild dogs, 42–3, 50, 59
wildebeest, 58, 59
wings, 18, 33, 49, 52
wolves, 14, 32, 42–3, 52, 58
woodpeckers, 16

Credits

The publisher thanks Alexandra Cooper for her contribution, and Puddingburn for the index.

ILLUSTRATIONS
Front cover Christer Eriksson; **back cover tr** Leonello Calvetti,
bc Kim Thompson/Kingpin; **bl** Ian Jackson/Kingpin; **spine** Simone End

Leonello Calvetti 5, 32–33, 52–53 **Christer Eriksson** 6–7, 16–17, 18–19,
42–43 **Gary Hanna** 5, 54–55, 56–57, 60, 61 **Ian Jackson/Kingpin** 1, 4, 5,
8–9, 20–21, 28–29, 34–35, 38–39, 40–41, 60, 61 **MBA Studios** 4, 26–27,
50–51 **James McKinnon** 10–11, 58–59 **Yvan Meunier Contact Jupiter** 3, 4,
22–23, 30–31 **Mick Posen/The Art Agency** 5, 36–37, 44–45, 46–47,
48–49, 60 **Claude Thivierge/Contact Jupiter** 4–5, 12–13, 16, 18, 61, 62–63
Kim Thompson/Kingpin 14–15, 32, 60, 61

Additional support illustrations by: Jane Beatson, Martin Camm,
Simone End, Marjorie Crosby Fairall, Ray Grinaway, Tim Hayward/
Bernard Thornton Artists UK, Dr. David Kirshner, Robert Morton,
Barbara Rodanska, Chris Shields/The Art Agency, Roger Swainston

MAP ILLUSTRATIONS Andrew Davies

PHOTOGRAPHS
Key t=top; l=left; r=right; tl=top left; tcl=top center left; tc=top center;
tcr=top center right; tr=top right; cl=center left; c=center; cr=center
right; b=bottom; bl=bottom left; bcl=bottom center left; bc=bottom
center; bcr=bottom center right; br=bottom right

APL=Australian Picture Library; NPL=Nature Picture Library;
NHPA=Natural History Photographic Agency; PL=photolibrary.com

10t APL; **20bl** NHPA; **26bl** NPL; **28tr** NHPA; **32br** PL; **46c** NHPA; **50br cr** PL; **60tc** PL